M.Synge

Collected Works I
POEMS

J. M. SYNGE: COLLECTED WORKS

General Editor: ROBIN SKELTON

POEMS

J. M. SYNGE

COLLECTED WORKS

Volume I

POEMS

EDITED BY

ROBIN SKELTON

1982

COLIN SMYTHE

GERRARDS CROSS, BUCKS

THE CATHOLIC UNIVERSITY OF
AMERICA PRESS

WASHINGTON, D.C.

Copyright © 1962 Oxford University Press

This edition published in 1982
by Colin Smythe Limited, Gerrards Cross,
Buckinghamshire

British Library Cataloguing in Publication Data

Synge, John Millington
The collected works of J. M. Synge
Vol. 1: Poems
I. Skelton, Robin
822'.9'12   PR5530

ISBN 0–86140–134–4
ISBN 0–86140–058–5 Pbk.

First published in North America in 1982
by The Catholic University of America Press, Washington, D.C.

ISBN 0–8132–0563–8
ISBN 0–8132–0562–x Pbk.

Library of Congress Catalog Card No. 82–70362

CONTENTS

INTRODUCTION

THE poetry of J. M. Synge is not usually regarded as being the most important part of his literary output, and with some reason. It is, however, unfortunate that the impressiveness of his plays has so often blinded people to the power and originality of the best of his poems. The verses which were published in 1909 and 1910 are not only admirable, but also important from an historical point of view, in that they had a considerable influence upon W. B. Yeats, and also upon much English and Irish poetry of the twentieth century. It is high time that as complete a collection of Synge's poems as is reasonable should be published in order both to document his 'poetic progress' and to bring into the light many good poems which have not previously been available for consideration. This edition is, therefore, not only an attempt at providing a definitive canon of Synge's work as a poet, but also an attempt to show something of his methods of composition and of the gradual development of his work over the years.

It is not necessary to provide a biography of Synge in this book. The biography by David H. Greene and Edward M. Stephens is available for any reader who wishes for an account of his life. This book was created by Professor Greene out of a long typescript biography by the late Edward M. Stephens, Synge's nephew, and from other material taken from Synge's notebooks, manuscripts, and letters, and is as detailed as most readers would require. Certain facts, however, are particularly relevant to the understanding of Synge's development as a poet, and it might be as well to mention some of them here.

Synge was born in 1871 at Rathfarnham, Co. Dublin, which was then in the country, and not the suburb it is now. He spent most of his boyhood in the countryside, and was passionately interested in ornithology. Indeed, his first 'literary composition' is a nature diary he made in collaboration with Florence Ross when they were children together. It is not surprising, therefore, that his very earliest poems are somewhat Wordsworthian in tone. Wordsworth was still his favourite poet in 1894, and his enthusiasm for his work was shared by Cherry Mattheson, with whom he fell in love.

The relationship with Cherry Mattheson was not successful, and the break between them was finally made in October 1896. It was this unhappy love affair, together with other, less certainly known, relationships which lay behind Synge's first attempt at a poetic 'opus' of any size. This was *Vita Vecchia*, a series of poems linked together by a prose narrative in which Synge retold in a disguised form various of his experiences and yearnings. At the same period he composed an equally fictionalized and morbid autobiographical sketch. In the original version of *Vita Vecchia* there are fourteen poems, some of which were certainly written before 1896. Synge later revised this work, cutting out all the prose, and several of the poems, and re-ordering the remainder. The existing copy of this second version contains eight poems numbered 1 and 3–9. A number 2 may at some time have existed, but this is no longer certain. One of these eight poems was, later still, completely rewritten, and both the revised and the rewritten versions are included in this edition.

Vita Vecchia was completed first in Paris, and can be regarded as central to Synge's poetic attitudes at this period. After the turn of the century, however, the tone of his work changed, and in 1902 he concerned himself very largely with the problem of writing poetic drama. Unfortunately he destroyed all but a few fragments of the plays he completed, and so this aspect of his poetry is not well represented in this edition. I have, indeed, only chosen to print those fragments of two plays which Synge himself thought worthy of preservation, and a typical fragment from an early draft of a third. More material will be printed in Dr. Saddlemyer's forthcoming edition of the plays, where it perhaps more properly belongs. It was Synge's dramatic work, however, which led, somewhat obliquely perhaps, to the writing of many of his later poems. In 1906 he became friendly with Molly Allgood, a young actress who was the sister of Sarah Allgood and who is better known as Maire O'Neill, and they later became engaged. A great many of the poems Synge wrote from 1906 onwards were either about his love affair, or sent to his fiancée in letters. It is certain that she encouraged his work as a poet, and it may have been her encouragement which led him, in 1907, to contemplate the publication of some of his poems. He revised many of them at this time, and even drafted a preface in one of his notebooks. This preface runs:

In publishing the following verses and sketches I am doing what I have sometimes decided it would be better to leave undone. They were written from five to eight years ago and, as is obvious enough, in Paris among all the influences of the so-called decadent and symbolist schools. Still I think as a man has no right to kill one of his children if it is diseased or insane, so a man who has made the gradual and conscious expression of his personality in literature the aim of his life, has no right to suppress himself any carefully considered work which seemed good enough when it was written suppression if it is deserved will come rapidly enough from the same causes that suppress the unworthy members of a man's family. To burn what one has written without giving at least one chance of existence is a sort of intellectual suicide against which ones instinct crys out, and if as in the present the piece were written some years ago, we the chances always are that the writer himself is no longer suited to judge what he has written. At the moment of creation the balance of the critical and creative impulses which works in the forming of any artistic production is the essential artistic element of the writers temperament at that moment. To let his critical judgement of thirty five overthrow his creative impulse of twenty five is a quite different thing, and one which is only, if ever, quite justifiable in the case of work which appears to the maturer mind whole bad from a technical point of view. That is not so in my present judgement of what is now printed. I have matters which I wrote from 15 to 25 which I have burned because it seemed to me inarticulate and without a real literary existence. The same may be true of the present productions but if it is, there is a certain possibility or inevitable whether it be or no, which make it well to let these verses and studies make their own appeal to the only court which in arts dont not often err—the

Synge's handwriting (not to mention spelling and punctuation) was always erratic, and the phrase 'decadent and symbolist schools' in this draft might well be read, as Edward Stephens read it, as 'descendants of the symbolist schools'. He also read 'unworldly' where I read 'unworthy'. Such difficulties frequently occur in reading Synge's manuscripts, and it is a difficulty of which Synge himself was well aware. In the same notebook as the draft preface there is a note: 'I'm a good scholar at reading but a blotting kind of writer when you give me a pen—J. M. S.' It is appropriate that the reading 'blotting' must be considered conjectural.

In another notebook of the same period Synge made some rough notes upon the kind of poetry he most prized.

No one is less fond of theories and divisions in the arts than I am, and yet they cannot altogether be done without. In these matters we need not expect to say anything very new but in applying for ourselves to our own life what is thought in different ways by many we likely to hit on matters of some value. For a long time I have felt that

Poetry roughly is of two kinds the poetry of real life—the Poetry of Burns, and Shakespeare, Villon, and the poetry of a land of the fancy—the poetry of Spenser and Keats and Ronsard. That is obvious enough, but what is highest in poetry is always reached where the dreamer is leaning out to reality or where the man of real life is lifted out of it. and in all the poets the greatest have both these elements that is they are supremely engrossed with life and yet with the wildness of their fancy they are always passing out of what is simple and plain. Such is the case with Dante and Chaucer and Goethe and Shakespere. In Ireland Mr Yeats one of the poets of the fairyland has interests in the world and for this reason his poetry has had a lifetime in itself, but A. E. on the other hand who is of the fancyland only ended his career in poetry in his first volume

It would be easy to carry this division a long way. To compare the romances of the Arthurian style with the modern realistic novel, Gottfried of Strasburg and Molay become real here and there and then they are then extraordinarily powerful. So on the other hand it is only with Huysmans that the realistic became of interest

And, on the otherwise blank page opposite: 'Sudden in the romance writer a real voice seems to speak out of their golden and burning words, it is then they are greatest.'

Synge did not carry out his project of publishing the early poems in the fashion his draft preface suggests, and included only a few of his earliest productions in the selection of poems he sent to Yeats in 1908.

The letter accompanying the manuscript read in part as follows:

Dear Yeats,

Roberts wants me to give him the enclosed verses for publication. I read them to him the other day and he seemed taken with them. I would be grateful if you would look through them and let me know what you think. I do not at times feel sure of them, at other times I feel it would be better to print them now while I am alive, than to leave them after me to go God knows where. There are a few of them at least that I would not like to destroy.

If I print them I would possibly put a short preface to say that as there has been a false 'poetic diction' there has been and is a false 'poetic material'. That if verse, even great verse is to be alive it must be occupied with the whole of life—as it was with Villon and Shakespeare's songs, and with Herrick and Burns. For although exalted verse is the highest, it cannot keep its power unless there is more essentially vital verse at the side of it as ecclesiastical architecture cannot remain fine, when domestic architecture is debased. Victor Hugo and Browning tried in a way to get life into verse but they were without humour which is the essentially poetic quality in what I call vital verse.

George Roberts was the manager of Maunsel & Co., the Dublin publishers. This letter, like the great majority of Synge's manuscripts, was undated, but must have been written in August or early September, as Yeats's reply reached Synge on 8 September.

The National Theatre Society, Ltd.,
Abbey Theatre, Dublin.

Monday.

My Dear Synge:

Can you come and see me on Wednesday afternoon at Nassau (say) three o'clock. Some of the poems are very fine I want to talk about them. 'Well of Saints' had a fine reception tonight.

Yours—
W. B. YEATS

I go to Galway on Thursday.

The next day Synge wrote to Molly Allgood:

Wednesday Sept. 9/08

Dearest

Your letter came last night just in time to save you from another scolding! I got a letter from Yeats yesterday morning to say that some of the poems were *very fine* (no less) and to ask me to go in today to talk about them so I am going in after dinner.

There is no record of what happened at this meeting, but it seems clear that the original idea of 1907 that Synge should have a collection of verse published by Maunsel and Roberts alone was shelved in favour of the production of a limited edition by the Cuala Press, to be followed by a larger trade edition from Maunsel & Co. in the course of time. Some light upon this is shed by a letter from George Roberts, Maunsel's manager, to Yeats on 18 October 1910, when they were in disagreement over what should be included in the four-volume edition of Synge's works. Roberts writes:

I must remind you of your action in the matter of the publication of the Poems; when Mr. Synge sent you his Manuscript (which he had already arranged with me to publish)—for your 'opinion', you held to it for the Cuala Press. Synge then came to me and said if it was a question of us OR the Cuala Press publishing them he would unhesitatingly go on with his original arrangement with us. But for your representing that your sister's press would be idle I would have looked to the interest of my own firm, which, of course, I had every right to do.

Some further revisions also appear to have been suggested, for on 2 October Synge wrote to Molly Allgood:

I handed over the M.S. of my poems to Yeats yesterday so I hope that will go alright now. I did one new poem—that is partly your work—that he says is *Magnificent*.

Three days later he signed a contract with Maunsel & Co. for the production of a trade edition, and the following day, 6 October, he set off for a holiday in Germany. His health was now extremely bad, and, in fact, he had only six months more to live.

He arrived back in Dublin on 7 November, his holiday having been cut short by his mother's death. During November he worked on the preface to his poems, and wrote several new ones. He sent a group of his poems to the *Nation*, but they were rejected. His health was getting worse, and he was suffering considerable pain from his stomach. Nevertheless he continued to work at his poems, and upon *Deirdre of the Sorrows*. Elizabeth Yeats wrote to him:

CUALA INDUSTRIES, LTD.
CHURCHTOWN, DUNDRUM, CO. DUBLIN
Nov 25 1908

Dear Mr Synge

Thank you very much for writing about the poems. The only two that I would like left out are 'The Curse' and 'Danny' I hope you don't think it silly of me to want them taken out?

The week after next we could begin setting up your book & we will send you proofs then we could print it immediately after Christmas—& it ought to be dry enough to bind & issue early in March. Will that be all right? In the circular we have just called the book 'Poems by J. M. Synge' & have made the subscription 10/6 We were all very sorry to hear of your sad loss—I hope you are gaining strength—It is very good of you to give us your book—Will it be all right if we give you a royalty of fifteen per cent on the book—I don't think we can afford more. I thought of making the edition 300 copies

With Kind regards
yours sincerely
ELIZABETH C. YEATS

The first proofs arrived in January. The two poems—'The Curse' and 'Danny'— had been omitted.

Cuala Industries,
Churchtown, Dundrum,
Co. Dublin
Jan 6th 1909.

Dear Mr Synge—

At last I am sending you the proofs. I hoped to have sent them before Christmas—but one of my girls was ill, and is only able to be back at work this week—and we had not enough type distributed to set up your poems.

The last part of the book is I expect all wrongly set up—I did not know how you wanted it set—so we just did it for a first proof as it was in the M.S.

I have put blank pages between some of the poems as the book looked too small—At first we had it set up with the poems running on close after one another, but that wouldn't do—as it made the book so very small—We thought of putting 'Three Love Lyrics'

xviii

'Ballad' etc. before the poems in red—What do you think—we can make any alteration you want—I enclose a stamped envelope for the return of proofs and I send two sets one for you to keep the other to send back to us—Above the word 'Preface' it might look well to repeat the title of the book? We have not yet set up title page and contents but will send it with the revise. I hope you are some-what better

Yours very sincerely

ELIZABETH C. YEATS

P.S. Of course these proofs are on very common paper—so do not look very well.

Synge's extreme reticence over his poems is illustrated by a story told in the immensely thorough and valuable type-script *Life* written by Edward M. Stephens, which was used by David H. Greene, after Mr. Stephens's death, as the basis of the Biography which bears the names of both of them. Edward Stephens wrote:

> When I called to see John one evening, the proofs that Miss Yeats had sent him were lying on the table. He showed them to me, and explained that he had put together a small collection of poems which might be lost if they were not published. Besides those in-cluded in the proofs, he said he had two more that Miss Yeats thought too strong for inclusion in the little book she was printing.
> He had never before mentioned to me that he had written poetry. His poems seemed so intimate that I was surprised at his willingness to publish them, and was so much embarrassed by his showing them to me that I could form no detached view of what I read. I did not know what to say, but he did not seem to expect me to say anything, and went on to talk about the publication of his book by Miss Yeats.

This reticence may, to some extent, have been reserved for his family, as Padraic Colum tells me that, though he cannot remember Synge's ever telling him that he wrote poetry, he had always assumed that poems existed. John Masefield, of course, knew of Synge's poems in 1907. Moreover, as early as 12 April 1908 Agnes Tobin was

xix

writing from San Francisco: 'My very best wishes for Easter. Has Deirdre completely swallowed you up? And when am I to have The Tinker's Wedding? Above all— when am I to have the Laura Sonnets in Folk Speech?' On 17 December of the same year she wrote from London: 'How can we possibly wait till March to see the volume of your poems! It is delightful to think of it.'

Synge returned the proofs almost immediately. Miss Yeats replied:

Gurteen Dhas,
Churchtown,
Dundrum,
Co. Dublin.

Thursday Jan. 8, 1909.

Dear Mr. Synge,

You are very quick over the proofs. The most stupid slip I let pass was making one line of 'When you have kissed me black and blue' —We are now making all your corrections and will send you a revise—it may take a little time as I am getting them to alter the arrangement of the pages getting the blocks of type to back better, it looks ugly at present.

We are very glad that you are a little better—I wish I knew whether it was wise (from a business point of view) to include 'The Curse' and 'Danny' but I don't really know—

Did you happen to notice what the postage on the MS. and proofs I sent you was—the post office here is making a lot of mistakes they charged 8½ and I want to investigate as they have made a heap of mistakes.

Yours sincerely,

E. C. YEATS.

Synge was now aware of the precarious condition of his life, and spent some time going through his manuscripts, marking some for future publication, and placing a ban upon others. Elizabeth Yeats wrote again on 20 January:

CUALA INDUSTRIES, LTD.,
CHURCHTOWN,
DUNDRUM, CO. DUBLIN.

Jan. 20.

You will wonder why I have not sent you a revise—I am waiting
a few days as we have to get two months Broadsides printed first—
and I sent Mr. Walker, the Doves Press the proofs of your book in
hopes he will make some suggestions. We will do it quickly when
we begin. E. Yeats.

Synge entered hospital on 2 February 1909. His nephew
Edward Stephens helped him get ready, and Synge showed
him his manuscripts and went through them with him.
Elizabeth Yeats wrote again on 3 February, enclosing a
letter from Emery Walker.

CUALA INDUSTRIES, LTD.,
CHURCHTOWN, DUNDRUM,
CO. DUBLIN.

Feb. 3. 1909.

Dear Mr. Synge,
    I suppose you have no more poems we could add to make the
book larger. You see Mr. Walker doesn't like the look of it any
more than I do—I enclose his letter—At first we tried it with the
poems running on close after one another but this makes the book
appear too small—
    The only other plan I can think of is to print the poems as they are
and then set the translations on a smaller measure so that they would
each more completely fill the page. Not knowing how to make the
book look well has bothered me—and we could begin to print it
next week—I am having a new parchment on the Press and want to
do everything I can to make the book look well—this Press is in use
this week printing the March Broadside but this will be done on
Friday and on Saturday we can try a proof with the prose on a nar-
rower measure. The italic headings to the prose will help. We could
put them in red ink—I went to T.C.D. Library on Monday   and
saw crowds of books hoping I would get some idea, but that didn't
throw any light on how best to arrange the book. More poems

would be the best solution as then we could set it by running or like 'In The Seven Woods' A.E.'s poems etc. We will do it quickly once we begin and we can begin at once now.

Yours sincerely,
ELIZABETH C. YEATS[1]

Mr. Walker had written:

14 Clifford's Inn,
Fleet Street
London E.C.
Jan. 22, 1909

Dear Lolly,

I am very sorry I have been such a long time answering your letter about Mr. Synge's little book. I am afraid the radical defect in it is that it is 'lumbed out too much. No book could possibly look well typographically that had so little print and so much white paper. Could you not set it closer? The prose pages look particularly badly as they are. But I don't think there is much hope of making it look a reasonable book unless you entirely recast it. If you must keep to this form, perhaps it would be better if you put the folios at the foot of each page in the centre—backing each other of course. I am afraid people may think it looks dear'.* How would it be, as it is all new and unpublished matter, to print a larger number and sell it at 5/-? Do you think you could print as many more as would pay you?

In answer to your letter of yesterday, we too have had the same bother at times with the paper going mouldy . . . etc etc

Yours sincerely,
EMERY WALKER.

* I asked if he thought it would be too dear at 10/6. [*Note in Elizabeth Yeats's hand.*]

Another letter from Elizabeth Yeats dated 11 Jan. 1909 seems to have been misdated and to fit into the pattern at this point.

[1] Yeats wrote in *The Death of Synge, and other Passages from an Old Diary* (1928): 'Last night my sister told me that this book of Synge's (his poems) was the only book they began to print on a Friday. They tried to avoid this but could not, and it is not at all well printed. Do all they could, it would not come right.'

Cuala Industries, Ltd.,
Churchtown, Dundrum, Co. Dublin.
Monday, Jan. 11, 1909.

Dear Mr. Synge,

Here is a revise. I don't think we have yet made it look right, but it is so difficult to judge on this horrid paper but if you will see if there are no mistakes we can see to the *arrangement of the printing on the page.* What would you like on the title page—just 'Poems by J. M. Synge.'?

Yours sincerely,
Elizabeth C. Yeats

On 13 February Synge made his will. On 18 February Miss Yeats wrote again.

CUALA INDUSTRIES, LTD.,
CHURCHTOWN, DUNDRUM,
CO. DUBLIN.
Thursday, Feb. 18, 1909.

Dear Mr. Synge,

I am thinking of putting a drawing as a frontispiece to your book—that is if you would like the idea. Jack has done me the enclosed. I send you his letter. My idea is that the subscribers may think 10/6 too much for so small a book and that a drawing would make it look more expensive—of course I think it should be a woodblock—so there are difficulties ahead yet—but I don't want to go on with the idea till I know if you approve or not; *say exactly what you think.*

The book is not really expensive compared to our 7/6 books as it is not a reprint and many of them were—I have gone through the proofs again and have found a few slips I ought to have found before —I enclose the proposed corrections—if you feel well enough could you let me know if I am to carry them out. We have printed the first eight pages.

I hope that you are much better.

Yours sincerely,
Elizabeth C. Yeats.

No drawing was published in the Cuala Press edition. J. M. Synge died at 5.30 in the morning of 24 March 1909. The Cuala Press completed the printing of his book on

8 April, including in it a long Introduction by W. B. Yeats. Thus Synge never saw his poems in book form. Indeed the only poem of his that he ever saw in print was the sonnet 'Glencullen' which appeared sixteen years earlier in the magazine of Trinity College, Dublin, when he was a student.

The Cuala Press Edition was limited to 250 copies. John Quinn published a private edition in America in the same year. This was limited to fifty copies. In both these books there were sixteen poems and eleven translations. *The Works of John M. Synge* was published by Maunsel in four volumes in 1910. The second volume included the poems and translations, and Yeats (who made the selection) added six more poems and six more translations, taking his material both from manuscripts set aside for the purpose by Synge, and from other manuscripts. No further poems or translations were published until 1959 when various poems and fragments were included in the text of the Greene and Stephens Biography, the Maunsel text being continually reprinted as a separate volume from 1911 onwards. Thus the canon of Synge's poems has remained almost unaltered for fifty years, the only other additions having been made in my own small limited edition of the Translations, published by the Dolmen and Oxford University Presses in 1961.

The present text is based upon the Cuala Press Edition, which Synge himself corrected in proof, upon the Maunsel text, and upon manuscript sources. The poems first printed in the Maunsel text have been checked, wherever possible, against the manuscripts. This was necessary, for Synge's manuscripts are not easy to edit, and I could not be absolutely certain that Yeats had not made mistakes, particularly as it is possible that he did not examine all the manuscript material now available.

It is necessary here to say a word about Synge's manuscripts. Synge's method of composition for both plays and poems was to rewrite continually. A poem is likely to begin in a notebook draft, continue through several typescript versions, be amended by several notebook jottings, and end up again in three or four typescripts, none of the different versions having been dated. Moreover, if one may judge from purely internal evidence, it appears that occasionally version 5 would be scribbled on the back of a typescript of version 2, and version 3, because of lack of manuscript corrections to the typescript, would look like the final version. The notebooks, admittedly, do contain some dated material, but these dates are not always as helpful as they might appear, as Synge was quite as likely to scribble a poem of 1902 in a notebook containing material of 1897 as he was to transcribe an early poem into a later notebook. To add to this confusion, Synge's handwriting after about 1898 did not alter sufficiently for it to be of much help in determining dates of composition.

This has made the job of editing the poems rather difficult, and in many cases I must admit that my dating is more conjectural than I should like. I have, however, tried wherever possible to give the year in which each poem was begun, and also, where late revision took place, the year in which the poem achieved the form in which it was, or is now, first published. I have not attempted to give variant manuscript readings of all the poems, but wherever there is some doubt over which version is the latest, or wherever the variants appear to me to be particularly interesting, I have documented the poem as fully as seems sensible. Where Synge did not provide a title to his poem I have myself invented one, and printed it in brackets, in order to facilitate reference. The only exception to this is the series of translations from Petrarch, where I have left

Synge's numbering. In two cases I have devoted appendixes to work-sheets. The first appendix is devoted to the poem which I have called 'Is it a Month', the reason being that there is considerable doubt as to which version should be regarded as the final one. The second appendix I have devoted to 'In Kerry', partly because this poem illustrates Synge's working methods more fully than any other, and partly because the information already published about it (see the Biography, p. 139) is misleading. It is suggested, perhaps unintentionally, by referring to the poem in connexion with Synge's visit to Kerry in 1903, that the poem was begun then, whereas it was certainly begun in 1907.

The biography is not, unfortunately, altogether reliable concerning J. M. Synge's poetry. Although Edward Stephens's typescript is immensely accurate in its transcriptions of manuscript material, and completely reliable in matters of fact, having the lucidity and precision which one might expect from the work of a legally trained mind, some of the material appears to have been awkwardly handled in the editorial and redactory process of making a short biography from the vast amount of material which Mr. Stephens left behind him. I have, therefore, included in my notes to the poems which also appear in the biography details of those variations in readings which ought to be recorded in order to preserve Synge's text from multiplications of error by future commentators.

It is, of course, always difficult to decide whether or not to correct an author's misspelling or errors of punctuation. I have, in this edition, attempted to follow two principles. First of all, I have left Synge's punctuation exactly as I have found it, save for one or two cases where I have indicated my alteration in the notes. For the most part the punctuation does not, in these manuscripts, seriously affect the intelligibility of the poems. As regards spelling, I have only corrected spelling mistakes when these were grossly obvious as such, and interfered with the easy reading of the poem concerned. Where there was any faint possibility of regarding Synge's spelling as a legitimate variant, or as a deliberate gesture, I have allowed the manuscript version to stand. The only serious editorial privilege I have allowed myself is the substituting of names for initials in the fragments of the verse dramas, but only (of course) when it was clear what the initials in the manuscript implied. I have also changed Synge's occasional inconsistent spelling of Luamad for Luasnad and Lacne for Laine.

I must here indicate the nature of the manuscript sources for the text. These are mainly two. Synge kept notebooks all his life, and though few final versions exist in notebook form, they are important for early work, and for dating. The notebooks comprise my first source. My second source has been the vast amount of manuscripts Synge left behind him. These can be roughly grouped as follows:

(*a*) manuscript and typescript drafts of the already published plays and prose works;

(*b*) various files devoted to unpublished work and to published and unpublished poems.

It is not possible to use much of this second category of manuscript material with any real reliance upon the headings the various files are given, as even the most cursory examination of the material reveals that, over the years, manuscripts have become misplaced, and the contents of the files altered. Certain files were clearly created by Synge, but I cannot be certain that they have remained in the condition in which he left them. Thus a file marked 'Reserved Poems (Duplicates) 1906–1908 and Earlier' in Synge's hand is far from being a duplicate of a file marked 'Reserved Poems 1906–1908'. A file marked 'Biographical

Matter only not to be printed as literary work' may or may not have been created by Synge, but as some of the typescripts included in it are of earlier versions of 'In Kerry' than that of which Synge finally approved, it seems that it would be unwise to feel certain of its origin. Moreover, the file originally marked by Synge 'Poems for Maunsel's Edition' does not quite live up to its label either.

I mention this in order to explain that, where I refer to a file by name, it is not to be supposed that the title is given for any other reason than indicating the precise geographical source of my text. The notebooks, which have recently been catalogued and numbered by Dr. Ann Saddlemyer, are referred to by their numbers for the same reason. All the material used in the making of this edition of the poem is, of course, in the hands of the Synge Estate.

A further source, rather of elucidation of texts than of texts themselves, has been Mr. Edward Stephens's type-script *Life of Synge*, in which he accomplished astonishing feats of transcription. In one or two cases where his reading has conflicted with my own, and where Synge's handwriting has made it a purely arbitrary matter to decide which version is superior, I have given both versions.

In making this edition I have been greatly helped by a number of people in many ways. Edward Stephens's widow, Mrs. Lily M. Stephens, allowed me to make use of her home, and to consult her late husband's notes, transcripts, and typescript biography, and, together with Professor J. L. Synge, representing the heirs of the Synge estate, gave me every possible help. I am also indebted to Dr. Ann Saddlemyer for much helpful advice, and to Mr. J. Hurst, the Deputy Librarian of Trinity College, for some valuable information. The Director of the National Library of Ireland has been more than kind in allowing me to examine material in the Library's keeping. I must also thank the inhabitants of the National City Bank, Dublin, for allowing me to disrupt their lives by working on the manuscripts in their offices.

ROBIN SKELTON

Manchester University

PREFACES TO THE FIRST EDITION

JOHN M. SYNGE

The Lonely returns to the Lonely, the Divine to
the Divinity.   PROCLUS

I

WHILE this work was passing through the press Mr. J. M
Synge died. Upon the morning of his death one friend o
his and mine though away in the country, felt the burder
of some heavy event, without understanding where or fo
whom it was to happen; but upon the same morning on
of my sisters said, 'I think Mr. Synge will recover, for las
night I dreamed of an ancient galley labouring in a storm
and he was in the galley, and suddenly I saw it run int
bright sunlight and smooth sea, and I heard the keel grat
upon the sand.'[1] The misfortune was for the living certainly, that must work on, perhaps in vain, to magnify th
minds and hearts of our young men, and not for the dea
that having cast off the ailing body is now as I believe, al
passionate and fiery, an heroical thing. Our Daimon is a
dumb as was that of Socrates, when they brought in th
hemlock; and if we speak among ourselves, it is of th
thoughts that have no savour because we cannot hear hi
laughter, of the work more difficult because of the strengt
he has taken with him, of the astringent joy and hardnes
that was in all he did, and of his fame in the world.

[1] Cf. 'On the morning when I heard of his death a heavy storm wa
blowing and I doubt not when he died that it had well begun. That mornin
Lady Gregory felt a very great depression and was certain that some ev
was coming but feared for her grandchild, feared it was going to be ill. O
the other hand, my sister Lolly said at breakfast, "I think it will be all righ

Last September he wrote to me as follows.

Dear Yeats,

Roberts wants me to give him the enclosed verses for publication. I read them to him the other day and he seemed taken with them, and I would be very grateful if you would let me know what you think about it. I do not feel very sure of them; yet enough of myself has gone into them to make me sorry to destroy them, and I feel at times it would be better to print them while I am alive than to leave them after me to go God knows where.

If I bring them out I would possibly write a short preface to say that as there has been a false 'poetic diction' so there has been and is a false 'poetic material'; that if verse is to remain a living thing it must be occupied, when it likes, with the whole of a poet's life and experience as it was with Villon and Herrick and Burns; for though exalted verse may be the highest, it cannot keep its power unless there is more essentially vital verse—not necessarily written by the same man—at the side of it.

You will gather that I am most interested now in my grimmer verses, and the ballads (which are from actual life.) There is a funny coincidence about 'The Curse' you will find among them. . . .

Excuse this disjointed production; I cannot write letters with a type-writer: and please let me know your opinion as soon as you can. If I print them I might put some of my Petrarch translations into the book also, to make it a little less thin.

Yours ever

J. M. Synge.[1]

with Synge, for last night I saw a galley struggling with a storm and then it got into calm and bright sunlight and I heard the keel grate on the shore." One remembers the voyages to Tir-nan-oge, certainly the voyages of souls after death to their place of peace.' W. B. Yeats, *The Death of Synge and Other Passages from an Old Diary* (1928).

'My sister Lily says that the ship Lolly saw on the night of Synge's death was not like a real ship, but like the "Shadowy Waters" ship on the Abbey stage, a sort of allegorical thing. There was also a girl in a bright dress, but she seemed to vanish as the ship ran ashore; all about the girl, and indeed everything, was broken and confused until the bow touched the shore in bright sunlight.' *Ibid.*

[1] It will be noticed that the text of this version of Synge's letter differs in

The full title of 'The Curse' is 'To a sister of an enemy of
the author's who disapproved of The Playboy'.

> Lord, confound this surly sister,
> Blight her brow with blotch and blister,
> Cramp her larynx, lung, and liver,
> In her guts a galling give her.
> Let her live to earn her dinners
> In Mountjoy with seedy sinners.
> Lord, this judgement quickly bring,
> And I'm your servant, J. M. Synge.

He was persuaded to leave these lines out of this edition
of the poems, but what he says about the rough poems that
give weight to the more ecstatic, justifies me in restoring
it. In his Preface he speaks of these poems as having been
written during the last sixteen or seventeen years, though
the greater number were written very recently, and many
during his last illness. 'An Epitaph' and 'On an Anniversary'
show how early the expectation of death came to him, for
they were made long ago. But the book as a whole is a fare-
well written when life began to slip from him.

He was a reserved man, and wished no doubt by a vague
date to hide when still living what he felt and thought
from those about him. I asked one of the nurses in the
hospital where he died if he knew he was dying, and she
said, 'He may have known it for months, but he would
not have spoken of it to anyone.'[1] Even the translations of
some respects from that given earlier. The previous version was taken from
a transcript by Edward Stephens. It appears that Yeats could not resist the
temptation to 'improve' Synge's statements.

[1] Cf. 'March 24th. Synge is dead. In the early morning he said to the nurse
"It is no use fighting death any longer" and he turned over and died. . . . I
called at the hospital this afternoon and asked the assistant matron if he
knew he was dying. She answered, "He may have known it for weeks, but
he would not have said so to anyone. He would have no fuss. He was like
that." She added, with emotion in her voice, "We were devoted to him."'
W. B. Yeats, *The Death of Synge and Other Passages from an Old Diary* (1928)

poems that he has made his own by putting them into that melancholy dialect of his, seem to express his emotion at the memory of poverty and the approach of death. The whole book is of a kind almost unknown in a time when lyricism has become abstract and impersonal.

III

Now and then in history some man will speak a few simple sentences which never die, because his life gives them energy and meaning. They affect us as do the last words of Shakespeare's people that gather up into themselves the energy of elaborate events, and they in their turn put strange meanings into half-forgotten things and accidents, like cries that reveal the combatants in some dim battle.

Often a score of words will be enough, as when we repeat to ourselves, 'I am a servant of the Lord God of War and I understand the lovely art of the Muses', all that remains of a once famous Greek poet and sea rover. And is not that epitaph Swift made in Latin for his own tomb more immortal than his pamphlets, perhaps than his great allegory? 'He has gone where fierce indignation will lacerate his heart no more.' I think this book too has certain sentences, fierce or beautiful or melancholy, that will be remembered in our history, having behind their passion his quarrel with ignorance, and those passionate events, his books.

But for the violent nature that strikes brief fire in 'A Question', hidden though it was under much courtesy and silence, his genius had never borne those lion cubs of his. He could not have loved had he not hated, nor honoured had he not scorned; though his hatred and his scorn moved him but seldom, as I think, for his whole nature was lifted up into a vision of the world, where hatred played with the grotesque, and love became an ecstatic contemplation of noble life.

He once said to me, 'We must unite asceticism, stoicism, ecstasy; two of these have often come together but not all three:'[1] and the strength that made him delight in setting the hard virtues by the soft, the bitter by the sweet, salt by mercury, the stone by the elixir, gave him a hunger for harsh facts, for ugly surprising things, for all that defies our hope. In 'The Passing of the Shee' he is repelled by the contemplation of a beauty too far from life to appease his mood; and in his own work, benign images ever present to his soul must have beside them malignant reality, and the greater the brightness the greater must the darkness be. Though like 'Usheen after the Fenians' he remembers his master and his friends, he cannot put from his mind coughing and old age and the sound of the bells. The two blind people of 'The Well of the Saints' arise from the loveliness of their dreams to a foul reality; and that woman of 'The Shadow of the Glen' who 'was a hard girl to please' and is 'a hard woman to please' has to spend her life between a drunken tramp, an angry hateful husband, a young milksop, and a man who goes mad upon the hills. The old woman in 'The Riders to the Sea', in mourning for her six fine sons, mourns for the passing of all beauty and strength, while the drunken woman of 'The Tinker's Wedding' is but the more drunken and the more thieving because she can remember great queens. And what is it but desire of ardent life, like that of Usheen who cried 'tears down but not for God, but because Finn and the Fianna are not living;' that makes his young girls of 'The Playboy of

[1] Cf. 'In Paris Synge once said to me, "We should unite stoicism, asceticism and ecstasy. Two of them have often come together, but the three never." ' W. B. Yeats, *The Death of Synge and Other Passages from an Old Diary* (1928).

the Western World' prefer to any peaceful man their eyes have looked upon, a seeming murderer? Person after person in these laughing, sorrowful, heroic plays is 'the like of the little children do be listening to the stories of an old woman, and do be dreaming after in the dark night it's in grand houses of gold they are, with speckled horses to ride, & do be waking again in a short while and they destroyed with the cold, and the thatch dripping, maybe, and the starved ass braying in the yard.'

IV

It was only at the last in his unfinished 'Deirdre of the Sorrows' that his mood changed. He knew some twelve months ago that he was dying, though he told no one about it but his betrothed, and he gave all his thought to this play, that he might finish it. Sometimes he would despond and say that he could not; and then his betrothed would act it for him in his sick room, and give him heart to write again. And now by a strange chance, for he began the play before the last failing of his health, his persons awake to no disillusionment but to death only, and as if his soul already thirsted for the fiery fountains; there is nothing grotesque, but beauty only.

V

He was a solitary, undemonstrative man, never asking pity, nor complaining, nor seeking sympathy but in this book's momentary cries: all folded up in brooding intellect, knowing nothing of new books and newspapers, reading the great masters alone: and he was but the more hated because he gave his country what it needed, an unmoved mind where there is a perpetual last day, a trumpeting, and coming up to judgment.

W. B. Yeats.   April 4, 1909.

PREFACE

I HAVE often thought that at the side of the poetic diction, which everyone condemns, modern verse contains a great deal of poetic material, using poetic in the same special sense. The poetry of exaltation will be always the highest, but when men lose their poetic feeling for ordinary life, and cannot write poetry of ordinary things, their exalted poetry is likely to lose its strength of exaltation, in the way men cease to build beautiful churches when they have lost happiness in building shops.

Many of the older poets, such as Villon and Herrick and Burns, used the whole of their personal life as their material, and the verse written in this way was read by strong men, and thieves, and deacons, not by little cliques only. Then, in the town writing of the eighteenth century, ordinary life was put into verse that was not poetry, and when poetry came back with Coleridge and Shelley, it went into verse that was not always human.

In these days poetry is usually a flower of evil or good, but it is the timber of poetry that wears most surely, and there is no timber that has not strong roots among the clay and worms. Even if we grant that exalted poetry can be kept successful by itself, the strong things of life are needed in poetry also, to show that what is exalted, or tender, is not made by feeble blood. It may almost be said that before verse can be human again it must learn to be brutal.

The poems which follow were written at different times during the last sixteen or seventeen years, most of them before the views just stated, with which they have little to do, had come into my head.

The translations are sometimes free, and sometimes almost literal, according as seemed most fitting with the form of language I have used.

Glenageary, December 1908   J. M. S.

PART ONE

THE POEMS

Glencullen

O RIVER could'st thou make response in words
What questions I should ask of olden time!
What stories hear of daring deed and crime,
Of those who dwelt out here among their herds,
Feasting on plenteous beef, with milk and curds,
And then, beside thy softly mellowed chime,
Shouting exhultingly a martial rhyme
That rose spontaneous as a charm of birds,
But changes since have crept o'er all thy glen
And now a thrifty nation needs must strive
To grow rich wheat where nought then lived but
        game
Yet on the bank still sings the merry wren
And in thy stream the frolic ousels dive
While old traditions linger in thy name.

Written 1892. Published in *Kottabos*, Hilary Term 1893.

A Mountain Creed

A MOUNTAIN flower once I spied,
A lonely height its dwelling,
Where winds around it wailed and sighed
Sad stories sadly telling.

'Fair flower,' said I, 'thou all alone
'Thy days up here art spending,
'Now listening to the sad winds' moan
'And now before them bending.

'When clouds and mists infold thee round
'For many days together
'And o'er thee weep until the ground
'Is murky as the weather,

'I fear thy life is lone and sad,
'Thy soul encased in sorrow,
'Thou hast no songs to make thee glad;
'No bees come here to borrow

'Tell me the secret of thy life,
'Thy very soul's religion,
'That I may know the hope and strife
'That fill this dreary region.'

'My life is lonely as the sea,'
It softly made reply,
'But not so sad as seems to thee
'Or I should quickly die.

'I live not here to pine and mourn
'O'er what is not my making,
'But to fulfil my fate inborn
'And hold myself unquaking.

4

'Though gloomy cloud and storms of might
'Are not forever raging,
'And times there come of calm delight
'My weary woes assuaging;

   'Yet cloud and storm can hurt me not,
'My joy it is not pleasure,
'But 'tis to be, no humble lot,
'One jewel 'mid God's treasure.'

Written 1892. Unpublished.
Stanzas 1 and 7 appear in the Greene and Stephens Biography.

(*The Creed*)

MY thinking clear, soul powerful, my sight
The wealth of sun, moon, sea, cloud-vesture drains,
The loneliness of heather breathes delight,
I court steep streamlets, withered woods, and lanes.

For my own soul I would a world create,
A Christless creed, incredulous, divine,
With Earth's young majesty would yearning mate,
The arms of God around my breast intwine.

Written, probably, in the 1890's. Unpublished.

In a New Diary

WHAT records will this new year write
Upon these pages crisp and clear,
Will courage mark them with her might
Or leave them to the tones of fear?

Before these leaves are laid aside
To where their fellows crumpled lie,
Twelve months will pass in grief or pride
And marshal all the seasons by.

I start upon a stoney way
Untrod by feet of men
My strength or weakness to display
Until these leaves are sealed again.

Written 1892. Revised 1907? Unpublished.

The original draft in Notebook 4, in which several pieces of 1894–5 are written, contains seven stanzas. The dating 1892 on the later version, which appears to be Synge's own dating, may possibly be mistaken, therefore.

This notebook is inscribed, 'These boyish verses are *not* to be printed under any circumstances, J. M. S.', but Synge may have had second thoughts. The version above is taken from the file marked 'Biographical Matter only not to be printed as literary work'.

(Ballad of a Pauper)

'Good evenin Misther niver more
My face you'll see again
I'm so filled full of emptiness
So drownded with the rain

'That I'm jist goin' to the House
Jist goin' to be a pauper
To axe her gracious Majesty
For a life of meal and torper'

'Why ragged bones twere better choose
A schoolin in Glencree
Where you'd be taught a dacent thrade
With duds and eating free'

'There's none goes there but them as steals
I'm honester nor you,
I niver stole a staavin thef
As yous are proud to do!'

'This but the course of equity
We work for laws and right'
'Och Misther Horney spake the thruth
Your jobbers all for might!

'Well looked here young double phrase
If words are your desire,'—
'Its food I want great dunder head
Its cloths and meat and fire'

'Hold your whist you graceless imp
And let me say my say—'
'It's I thats fagged wid waitin for't
I'm wastin night and day'

'If you adopt the pauper thrade
They pay with public gold
For all your keep till daddy Nick
Upon your life grab hold

'But if you my advice will heed
And just some thrifle steal
In some six years of strict Glencree
You'll quite a rouser feel'

'By Jabs I niver had beleeved
It was a Horney spoke
Your comin nice and easy on
Wid us young thinkin folk!

'Its deuced stiff a cove must steal
To grow an honest man
But Gob I'll do't if you think
It is the best I can!'

Written 1895? Unpublished.
The first five stanzas were printed in the Greene and Stephens Biography and there punctuated. This version differs from the one existing MS. version which is printed here in the following main particulars:

II. 4. 'meals and torpor'; IV. 3. 'I nevir stole, a starvin' thief,';
IV. 4. 'yours'; V. 3. 'Honey'; V. 4. 'You're'.

While 'torpor' is a sensible correction, the alteration of 'meal' to 'meals' affects the sense of the poem, and the alteration of 'staavin thef,' and 'yous' affects its quality as dialect. Greene's reading of 'Honey' can only be explained by his failing to understand that the word 'Horney' was, at this period, a Dublin dialect word meaning policeman. He suggested that the poem should be regarded as 'a debate in ballad style between an old man of the roads on his way to the poorhouse and the speaker, a young man from one of the big houses in Wicklow, presumably Synge himself' (Biography, p. 41). This notion explains his repunctuation of the fourth stanza, though it hardly explains the significance of the word 'yours'; 'yous' is perfectly acceptable dialect usage for 'you', and 'yours' makes nonsense in the context.

This poem is taken from Notebook 4. The fifth and sixth stanzas are crossed out.

(His Fate)

BY my light and only love
Long I lived in glee
Marked her musing deep delight
Murmur love for me

A footfall faint arose
Timid touched the way
Of one that many loved
In days passed away.

I faltered, found my feet
Bound me to her side
We wandered years and years
Till she drooped and died.

Written 1896. Unpublished.

From *Vita Vecchia*. The first poem of the original sequence. Not included in the revised version.

(At a Funeral Mass)

I HEARD low music wail
Woe wanton, wed to fear,
Heard chords to cleave and quail
Quelled by terror sheer.

I saw a woman bend,
Bowed in saintly prayer,
Where shadow round did wend,
Won by face so fair,

Like yours that kneeling form,
Far under mine that woe,
Our sorrow's rage and storm,
Stern gods had died to know.

Written 1896? Unpublished.

Synge attended a Funeral Mass at Saint Ignazio in Rome in 1896, and
Edward Stephens suggests that this poem originated there. On the
other hand, it was included in *Vita Vecchia*, as the fourth poem of the
original sequence, so it could have been written later.

In a Dream

I sAw thee start and quake,
When we in face did meet,
I saw dead passion wake,
One thrill of yearning sweet.

Then came a change, a wave,
Of bitterness, disdain,
That through my grassy grave
Will rack my haunted brain.

Written 1896. Revised 1907. Unpublished.

This revised version has 'bruise' as an alternative to 'rack', which appears as 'scourge' in the earlier version.

From *Vita Vecchia*. Originally the fifth poem in the sequence, but the third in the revised version. The title was given at the later date.

(*In Rebellion*)

THRICE cruel fell my fate,
Did I, death tortured, see,
A God, inhuman, great,
Sit weaving woes for me.

So hung as Hell the world,
Death's light with venom stung,
Toward God high taunts I hurled,
With cursing parched my tongue.

Written 1896. Revised 1907–8. Unpublished.

From *Vita Vecchia*. The thirteenth poem in the original sequence.
There is a variant of line 7: I taunts to Heaven hurled.

(*Execration*)

I CURSE my bearing, childhood, youth
I curse the sea, sun, mountains, moon,
I curse my learning, search for truth,
I curse the dawning, night, and noon.

Cold, joyless I will live, though clean,
Nor, by my marriage, mould to earth
Young lives to see what I have seen,
To curse—as I have cursed—their birth.

Written 1896–7. Unpublished.

From *Vita Vecchia*. Originally the sixth poem in the sequence, but the fourth in the revised version. The original manuscript has no comma after 'Nor', but does have a comma after 'earth'. I have repunctuated for the sake of clarity. The version in Notebook 25 is headed: 'My lady left me and I said'.

(*The Fugitive*)

I FLED from all the wilderness of cities,
And nature's choristers my art saluted,
Chanting aloud to me their tunes and ditties
And to my silent songs like joys imputed;

But when they heard me singing in my sorrow,
My broken voice that spoke a bosom breaking,
They fled afar and cried I Hell did borrow
As through their notes my notes fell discord waking.

Written July 1896. Revised 1907. Unpublished.

The earlier version has the line:
   'Chanting a Mass to me endite with ditties'.

From *Vita Vecchia*. Originally the seventh poem in the sequence, but the fifth in the revised version. Two lines of this poem occur in a notebook of 1902–3, so the poem may have suffered some revision before 1907.

In the City Again

WET winds and rain are in the street,
   Where I must pass alone,
Where no one wayfarer I meet
   That I have loved or known.

'Tis winter in my heart, the air
   Is wailing, bitter cold,
While I am wailing with despair,
   As I have wailed of old.

Written 1896. Revised c. 1907. Unpublished.

From *Vita Vecchia*. Originally the ninth poem in the sequence, but the sixth in the revised version. Synge completely rewrote this poem in 1908, and it was published under the title *Winter* in the Cuala Edition. This version appears on p. 63 of this edition.

(The Visitation)

I SAW among the clouds one woman white
Star-like descend. When I her aim descried
My temples reeled, I staggered, scarlet dyed,
Then sightless stood, heard, weeping, swift endite:—

'From Heaven have I seen thee, Wherefore here?
'I loved thee, named thee noble, praised thee pure,
'How canst thou to all lowness turn thee near,
'With loathsome life, how meditate, endure?'

I moaned, 'Sad, resolute, I torture flee:
'Him wouldst thou blame, joy-exiled, damned by
        thee?'

Written 1896. Revised 1907. Unpublished.

The earlier version is interesting: I have incorporated the MS. corrections to the typescript.

> Through ways I went where waned a lurid light,
> While round about lewd women wan did glide,
> (*Yet no hard hand I sought to soothe my side*)
> Yet none to my lone weeping I allied,
> But will-less went, held from the earth my sight:
> Then saw among the clouds one woman white
> Star-like descend; when I her aim descried
> My temples reeled, I staggered, scarlet dyed,
> Then sightless stood, heard weeping swift indite.

> 'From Heaven have I seen thee, wherefore here?
> 'I loved thee, named thee noble, praised thee pure,
> 'How canst thow to defilement turn thee near,
> 'How loathsome lust, thus tolerate, endure?'

> I moaned, 'Sad, innocent, I torture flee,
> 'Him wouldst thou blame, joy-exiled, damned by thee?'

From *Vita Vecchia*. Originally the tenth poem in the sequence, but the seventh in the revised version.

In Dream

AGAIN, again, I sinful see
　　Thy face, as men who weep
Doomed by eternal Hell's decree
　　Might meet their Christ in sleep.

Written 1896. Revised 1907. Unpublished.

An early version has the lines:

　　Eternal doomed by Hell's decree.
　　Might vision Christ in sleep.

From *Vita Vecchia*. Originally the eleventh poem in the sequence, but the eighth in the revised version. The title was added at the later date.

(The Conviction)

FIVE fives this year my years
Half life I live to dread,
Yet judged by weight of tears
Now were I calmed, were dead.

Yet this I hold as true.
That sleeping ends the strife
With death undying due
To soothe the pang of life.

Written 1896. Revised *c*. 1907. Unpublished.

An alternative version of line 6 reads:

There's sleep to end the strife

An earlier version included the stanza:

Not craven crushed in heart
Loves longing love decayed
I living learn my part
In sternness steeped arrayed

This followed the first stanza as above, and was followed by:

Yet bliss our credence new
That sleeping soothes the strife,
Annihilation due
To pall the pang of life.

From *Vita Vecchia*. Originally the twelfth poem in the sequence, but the ninth in the revised version.

(The Parting)

I STOPPED where you stood when you went you
    ways
And thought you would turn there never again
And my soul was sick where you went your ways
And dead if you never find it again

And I will wander and count the quais
By the church of our Lady beyond the Seine
Though my soul is sick of the countless quais
And the church of our Lady beyond the Seine.

Written 1898. Unpublished.

The manuscript, in a black notebook, has an uncancelled alternative
version of the fifth line. The whole line reads:

where you stood when
coin

re
I stopped at the rue   when   you went your ways

Rendez-vous Manqué dans la rue Racine

WHEN your hour was rung at last
I stood as in terror to watch the turn,
And met two creaking coffins that passed.
Lord God, I am slow to learn!

Written 1898. Revised 1906–8. Unpublished.

The 1898 version reads:

> I waited and walked in the Rue des Écoles
> And thought to see you arise from the West
> And many a rake and rouged troll
> Jeered my frozen zest
>
> And when your hour was rung at the last
> I stood with a shiver to watch the turn
> And met two creaking coffins that past
> Oh God! I am slow to learn.

L'Échange

'You are my God and my Heaven
Take me and my pearls and gold,
Yet leave me a franc for my souper,
My kitchen is rank with mould.'

She gathered my gold and my jewels,
Spangled her breast and head,
Yet I found when I sought my veau-piqué,
She had left me a franc of lead.

Written 1898. Revised 1906–8. Unpublished.

Various versions exist, none datable. The earliest version in a notebook
of 1898–9 has the variant readings:

    I. 3. Yet leave me vingt sous for my souper
    I. 4. My kitchen is green with mould.'
    II. 4. She had left me ten sous in lead

Other variants from various typescripts are:

    I. 3. Yet leave me a franc for my supper,
    I. 4. My rashers are green with mould
           The kitchen is bare and cold

    II. 3. Yet when I sought my veau-piqué
    II. 4. She had left me vingt sous in lead
            She had left me ten sous in lead

(Quatrain)

Is my love living to hold my hate
Or silently searching my soul with the dead
Would she forgive me or fool my fate
I loath the living to death I am wed!

Written 1899. Unpublished.

From the same notebook as an early version of 'L'Échange'.

(*At Dawn*)

RAINING came with dawning
Plastered our hair on our eyes,
Our agony gained with the daylight;
Our breathing cramped with cries;

Still we sat at the edge of the valley
Wet bat wings still beat at our ears
Till we dropped on the weeds that were withered
Scalding their roots with tears.

189-? Unpublished.

On another sheet of typescript is a variant stanza:

> Our agony gained with the daylight
> Wet bat-wings still beat at our ears,
> While we lay on the weeds that were withered
> Scalding their roots with tears

Stylistically this appears to be an early poem, but on the back of the
full version printed above are scribbled the lines:

> You've been eating bananas and whistling
> In my best and only chairs
> And kissing my cheeks though theyre bristling
> With black and with grisly hairs
> Your left profile is engaging
> I'm a hero seen from behind

These lines must have been written for Molly Allgood during
Synge's illness of 1907, when he had a minor operation on his neck.

It would be unwise, however, to accept this as an indication that
'At Dawn' was composed during this period. I have therefore placed
it among the poems of the 1890's.

(The Omission)

TODAY you have tutored and healed my head
Have taught me to see you and love you apart
But you have not forgiven the words I said
You have not renewed me the life of my heart

Written *c.* 1898. Unpublished.

(Three Sighs)

I KNOW the songs of the shower
Of thrush and pipit and wren
All the passionate flower
Of anguish in morbid men

Yet sweeter the sighs of your sighing
Three sighs half sighed for me
With lips that wrecked yet derided
The depth of my ecstasy.

189–? Unpublished.

There are alternative versions of lines 6 and 8 of this poem in an early copy:

        1. 6. Three sighs you sighed for me
                half sighed for my youth
        1. 8. The might of my ecstasy

The later version I have adopted has, as an alternative for the last word, 'Idiocy'.

(*In Spring*)

BUDS are opening their lips to the South
Sparrows are pluming their mates on the sill
Lovers are laying red mouth to mouth
Maidens are marging their smocks with a frill

Yet I lie alone with my depth of desire
No daughter of men would I choose for my mate
I have learned loving and lived to require
A woman the Lord had not strength to create

Written 1899. Unpublished.

Notre Dame des Champs

PIGEONS are cooing along the eaves
Grey flies are wooing their like on the leaves;

White-hood sisters sit at their prayer
With dronings that beat at my breast with the air;

The dust and the pavement are hot to my skin,
'Rise, little sisters, and let me in,

'You who are fragrant, and cool, and white,
Sisters of Mercy, to love is delight!'

Written 1899. Revised 1906–8. Unpublished.

Another and earlier version was printed in the Greene and Stephens Biography.

(The Serving Girl)

YOU are a peasant, mere maid by the day,
Humming in Gaelic sad songs while you dust,
I am a passer on paths of grey,
With a wallet half-worn for rhymes and a crust.

You who have eyes like stars lost in a wave,
A cadence to challenge dim nights of cloud,
I think you lean to my chant of the grave,
Will weave with my passion wild web for a shroud.

Written 1895–7? Revised 1902 and 1907? Unpublished.
This version is taken from a folder marked 'Reserved Poems (Duplicates) 1906–1908, and earlier. J. M. Synge.' It is marked 'Older, done in Paris', and attached to it are two poems of the 1890's. On the other hand, another version is included in a notebook of *c.* 1902, which contains the first draft of *Luasnad, Capa and Laine*. This version runs:

> You are a peasant—mere maid of an inn—
>   Humming in Gaelic white hymns while you dust
> While I am writing with torture thin
>   For a bushel of Gallic crust
>
> You have an eye bright to baffle the stars
>   You have the cadence of queens of cloud
> And think you I reckon the rood of bars
>   That pen the passive crowd

It seems not unlikely that the original version was written in Paris about 1895–7, revised in 1902, and further revised later—the latest revision finding its way into the file. This is, however, mere hypothesis.

To Ronsard

AM I alone in Leinster, Meath and Connaught
    In Ulster and the south,
To trace your spirit, Ronsard, in each song and sonnet
    Shining with wine or drouth?

How you were happy in your old sweet France
    Beside the Bellerie
Where you heard nymphs and Naiads wheel and
    dance
    In moon-light jovially.

Undatable. Unpublished.

Epitaph

A SILENT sinner, nights and days,
No human heart to him drew nigh,
Alone he wound his wonted ways,
Alone and little loved did die.

And autumn Death for him did choose,
A season dank with mists and rain,
And took him, while the evening dews
Were settling o'er the fields again.

189-? Published, Cuala Edn., 1909.

Prelude

STILL south I went and west and south again,
Through Wicklow from the morning till the night,
And far from cities, and the sites of men,
Lived with the sunshine and the moon's delight.

I knew the stars, the flowers, and the birds,
The grey and wintry sides of many glens,
And did but half remember human words,
In converse with the mountains, moors, and fens.

189–? Revised 1907. Published Cuala Edn., 1909.

The word 'sites' appears as 'sights' in the Maunsel and subsequent Editions. The Quinn Edition omits the second comma in the last line.

On an Anniversary

After reading the dates in a book of Lyrics.

WITH Fifteen-ninety or Sixteen-sixteen
We end Cervantes, Marot, Nashe or Green:
Then Sixteen-thirteen till two score and nine,
Is Crashaw's niche, that honey-lipped divine.
And so when all my little work is done
They'll say I came in Eighteen-seventy-one,
And died in Dublin . . . . What year will they write
For my poor passage to the stall of Night?

Undatable. Published, Cuala Edn., 1909.

According to Yeats this poem is an early one. Stylistically, it appears
to have more in common with the poems written after 1900 than
with those before. This may, however, be due to Synge's revision
of an earlier version now lost.

33

Queens

SEVEN dog-days we let pass
Naming Queens in Glenmacnass,
All the rare and royal names
Wormy sheepskin yet retains,
Etain, Helen, Maeve, and Fand,
Golden Deirdre's tender hand,
Bert, the big-foot, sung by Villon,
Cassandra, Ronsard found in Lyon.
Queens of Sheba, Meath and Connaught,
Coifed with crown, or gaudy bonnet,
Queens whose finger once did stir men,
Queens were eaten of fleas and vermin,
Queens men drew like Monna Lisa,
Or slew with drugs in Rome and Pisa,
We named Lucrezia Crivelli,
And Titian's lady with amber belly.
Queens acquainted in learned sin,
Jane of Jewry's slender shin:
Queens who cut the bogs of Glanna,
Judith of Scripture, and Gloriana,
Queens who wasted the East by proxy,
Or drove the ass-cart, a tinker's doxy,
Yet these are rotten—I ask their pardon—
And we've the sun on rock and garden,
These are rotten, so you're the Queen
Of all are living, or have been.

Written 1902. Published, Cuala Edn., 1909.

Early drafts occur in a notebook which contains material of 1902
and 1907, in a notebook of 1903, and in a small notebook of 1902.
The punctuation of this poem in the Maunsel Edn. differs from that of
this Cuala version.

On an Island

You've plucked a curlew, drawn a hen,
Washed the shirts of seven men,
You've stuffed my pillow, stretched the sheet,
And filled the pan to wash your feet,
You've cooped the pullets, wound the clock,
And rinsed the young men's drinking crock;
And now we'll dance to jigs and reels,
Nailed boots chasing girls' naked heels,
Until your father'll start to snore,
And Jude, now you're married, will stretch on the
    floor.

Written in 1905 or 1906. Published, Cuala Edn., 1909.

Patch-Shaneen

SHANEEN and Maurya Prendergast
Lived west in Carnareagh,
And they'd a cur-dog, cabbage plot,
A goat, and cock of hay.

He was five foot one or two,
Herself was four foot ten,
And he went travelling asking meal
Above through Caragh Glen.

She'd pick her bag of carrageen
Or perries through the surf,
Or loan an ass of Foxy Jim
To fetch her creel of turf.

Till on one windy Samhain night,
When there's stir among the dead,
He found her perished, stiff and stark,
Beside him in the bed.

And now when Shaneen travels far
From Droum to Ballyhyre
The women lay him sacks or straw,
Beside the seed of fire.

And when the grey cocks crow and flap,
And winds are in the sky,
'Oh, Maurya, Maurya, are you dead?'
You'll hear Patch-Shaneen cry.

Written 1907. Published, Cuala Edn., 1909.

There are early drafts of this poem alongside material of April-May
1907 in Notebook 33.

Beg-Innish

BRING Kateen-beug and Maurya Jude
To dance in Beg-Innish,
And when the lads (they're in Dunquin)
Have sold their crabs and fish,
Wave fawny shawls and call them in,
And call the little girls who spin,
And seven weavers from Dunquin,
To dance in Beg-Innish.

I'll play you jigs, and Maurice Kean,
Where nets are laid to dry,
I've silken strings would draw a dance
From girls are lame or shy;
Four strings I've brought from Spain and France
To make your long men skip and prance,
Till stars look out to see the dance
Where nets are laid to dry.

We'll have no priest or peeler in
To dance in Beg-Innish;
But we'll have drink from M'riarty Jim
Rowed round while gannets fish,
A keg with porter to the brim,
That every lad may have his whim,
Till we up sails with M'riarty Jim
And sail from Beg-Innish.

Written 1905 or 1906. Published, Cuala Edn., 1909.

The Passing of the Shee

After looking at one of A.E.'s pictures.

ADIEU, sweet Angus, Maeve and Fand,
Ye plumed yet skinny Shee,
That poets played with hand in hand
To learn their ecstasy.

We'll search in Red Dan Sally's ditch,
And drink in Tubber fair,
Or poach with Red Dan Philly's bitch
The badger and the hare.

Written 1907. Published, Cuala Edn., 1909.

Edward Synge's copy of the MSS. of an earlier version of this poem
which was sold 30/8/23 reads:

> Adieu, sweet Angus, Maeve and Fand,
> Ye plumed yet skinny Shee
> Our poets walked with hand in hand
> To learn fine ecstasy.
>
> We've learned to cherish Kerry men
> The ditches lovers know
> The badger, salmon, water hen
> The weazel lark and crow.

A still earlier version, which appears in Notebook 33 alongside
material of April–May 1907, ends fragmentarily but forcefully,

> For its better far to be a
> — — — — than patriot
> Rhyming reems of bloody rot.

Epitaph

After reading Ronsard's lines from Rabelais.

IF fruits are fed on any beast
Let vine-roots suck this parish priest,
For while he lived, no summer sun
Went up but he'd a bottle done,
And in the starlight beer and stout
Kept his waistcoat bulging out.

Then Death that changes happy things
Damned his soul to water springs.

Written 1907? Published, Cuala Edn.,

Dread

BESIDE a chapel I'd a room looked down,
Where all the women from the farms and town,
On Holy-days, and Sundays used to pass
To marriages, and Christenings and to Mass.

Then I sat lonely watching score and score,
Till I turned jealous of the Lord next door. . . .
Now by this window, where there's none can see,
The Lord God's jealous of yourself and me.

Written 1906–8. Published, Maunsel Edn., 1910.

The Stephens MS. suggests that the poem was completed in
January 1908, but a draft in Notebook 47 is dated 23.xi.08 in Synge's
hand. The final draft has 'In Desolate Humour' as an alternative title.
Another is called 'Beside a Chapel'. The Maunsel Edn. differs slightly
in punctuation from the MS. from which the above version is taken.

(*The Alteration*)

I KNEW all solitude, it seemed
That any man might know
Dead year met year, and then I dreamed
I might have comfort so.

But now when you and I apart
Must pass two days or three
Then in the desert of my heart
I perish utterly.

Written October 1906. Unpublished.

Samhain

THOUGH trees have many a flake
Of copper, gold, and brass,
And fields are in a lake
Beneath the withered grass;

Though hedges show their hips
And leaves blow by the wall
I taste upon your lips
The whole year's festival.

Written 1906–8. Unpublished.

(The Meeting)

WE met among the furze in golden mist,
Watching a golden moon that filled the sky,
And there my lips your lips' young glory kissed
Till old high loves, in our high love went by.

Then in the hush of plots with shining trees
We lay like gods disguised in shabby dress,
Making with birches, bracken, stars and seas,
Green courts of pleasure for each long caress;
Till there I found in you and you in me
The crowns of Christ and Eros—all divinity.

Written 1906. Unpublished.

Synge crossed out all of this poem but lines 5-8, but marked these
'Good & work up.'

What appears to be a much earlier version of this poem exists in a
notebook of 1906. This version probably refers to a walk taken with
Molly Allgood on 13 May 1906, according to the Stephens MS. It
runs:

> When the past twilight met a clouded moon
> And all the birds sang out a closing song
> On hilly paths that left the glens too soon
> Your feet with mine from Brittas passed along
>
> And when we stood in soft and golden mist
> To watch the silver silence of the sky
> My two glad lips your lips soft glory kissed
> Till God's great love in our great love went by
>
> Then all the young gay leaves and stars and birds
> Made in this rugged earth green courts of joy
> And we went walking through a maze of dreams
> Draining the fragrant night of Bonacroy.

(continued on p. 44)

And all we knew of quiver hymn and creeds
And old divinities construed by men
Flamed out when some strange moonbeam touched the reeds
Or sweet new scent upon our nostrils ran

Till we were left two gods in shabby dress
And made our Eden in the gold moon's light
Who while their arms grew tight for each caress

The unintelligible use of the word 'quiver' is probably the result
of Synge's changing his notions as he scribbled. Such oddities
occur not infrequently in the notebook drafts.

In Glenasmole

WE reached the Glen of Thrushes where Usheen
Lost all his youth and turned diseased and grey,
And there your lips—such lips few men have seen—
With one long kiss took my dead years away.

And then your young girl's voice grew wide and
    deep,
With happy words in love's long wisdom planned,
And all the glen grew dim with sunny sleep,
While brow met brow and hand met happy hand.

Written 1906? Unpublished.

This poem exists in several versions, all undated. One other completed version reads:

> We reached the glen where Finn's Usheen
> Lost youth and turned diseased and grey,
> And there your life and sap of green
> With kisses took my years away
>
> For this your voice grew wide and deep
> With words in love's long wisdom planned
> And all the glen grew dim with sunny sleep
> While brow met brow and hand each happy hand.

Another version reads:

> We reached the glen where Finn's Usheen
> Lost youth, and turned diseased and grey,
> And there your lips and cap of green
> With kisses won my years away.
>
> Your young girl's voice grew wide and deep
> With words in love's long wisdom planned,
> And all the glen grew dim with sleep
> In Tir na-n-óg, that lover's land

(continued on p. 46)

And a third, entitled *Tir-Na-Og*:

> In Glenasmoil where Finn's Usheen
>   Was aged one summer's day,
> Your lips and cap of gold and green
>   Enticed my years away
>
> And then your words grew wild and deep
>   In love's long wisdom planned
> And all the glen grew dim with sleep
>   In our Youth's Holy-Land.

To the Oaks of Glencree

MY arms are round you, and I lean
Against you, while the lark
Sings over us, and golden lights, and green
Shadows are on your bark.

There'll come a season when you'll stretch
Black boards to cover me:
Then in Mount Jerome I will lie, poor wretch,
With worms eternally.

Undatable. Published, Cuala Edn., 1909.
The Quinn Edn. omits the second comma in the third line.

In Glencullen

THRUSH, linnet, stare and wren,
Brown lark beside the sun,
Take thought of kestril, sparrow-hawk,
Birdlime, and roving gun.

You great-great-grand-children
Of birds I've listened to,
I think I robbed your ancestors
When I was young as you.

Undatable. Published, Cuala Edn., 1909.
The Quinn Edn. has the reading 'kestrel'.

The Curse

*To a sister of an enemy of the author's who
disapproved of 'The Playboy'*

LORD, confound this surly sister,
Blight her brow with blotch and blister,
Cramp her larynx, lung, and liver,
In her guts a galling give her.
Let her live to earn her dinners
In Mountjoy with seedy sinners:
Lord, this judgment quickly bring,
And I'm your servant, J. M. Synge.

Written 1907. Published in Yeats's Preface to the Cuala Edn., 1909.
The Playboy of The Western World was first performed on 26 January
1907. On 25 March 1907 Synge wrote to Molly Allgood: 'I have
written a lovely curse on the "flighty one" but I'm half afraid to
send it to you. . . .' The person cursed, according to the Greene and
Stephens Biography, 'was Molly's sister, Mrs. Callender, who had
expressed her dislike of *The Playboy*'.
    The earlier version of this poem printed in the Biography derives
from a draft written on two sides of one sheet of paper. These drafts
run:

(i)
                          female's fickle
          Lord curse this ~~womans flighty~~ *head*
          ~~Lord~~ *with gripes and*
                                grace
          Send her colics ~~in~~   *her bed*
               to cramp   burgeon round her
          Corns ~~to twinge~~ *her yellow toes*
          Send ~~her~~ *corns to cramp her*
          Inflame   spots
          Seven ~~pimples~~ *on her nose*
          Torment contort her waist with horrid
                          ears   pain
          Her teeth and ~~gums~~ *torment with*
          Contrive
          In every joint ~~contrive~~ *a sprain,*

49

for
May the devil in her sleep
Through her flesh with horrors creep
May her supper, breakfast, dinner
Choke   *flighty*
~~Rend~~ with wind his ~~curly~~ sinner
Lord these torments quickly bring
And I'm your servant J. M. Synge

(ii)

With corns and bunions cramp her toes
Deck with pimples brow and nose
Contort her liver lungs and brain
For all her parts contrive
                     a pain
Contrive for every inch
Till ~~ten~~ devils though she wake or sleep
Through her flesh with horror creep
Till her breakfast, supper, dinner

These drafts also suggest that the poem was not conceived as divisible into stanzas. The Maunsel version appears to follow the Cuala version in making the poem one of two stanzas, but, in fact, the split in the Cuala Edn. occurs because the poem is divided between two pages.

A Wish

MAY seven tears in every week
Touch the hollow of your cheek,
That I—signed with such a dew—
For a lion's share may sue
Of the roses ever curled
Round the May-pole of the world.

Heavy riddles lie in this,
Sorrow's sauce for every kiss.

Written 1907. Published, Cuala Edn., 1909.
An early version was included in a letter to Molly Allgood dated
26 March 1907. This version is quoted on p. 260 of the Greene and
Stephens Biography.

May one sorrow every day
Your festivity waylay.
May seven tears in every week
From your well of pleasure leak
That I—signed with such a dew—
May for my full pittance sue
Of the Love forever curled
Round the maypole of the world.

Heavy riddles lie in this,
Sorrow's sauce for every kiss.

(*Is it a Month*)

Is it a month since I and you
In the starlight of Glen Dubh
Stretched beneath a hazel bough
Kissed from ear and throat to brow,
Since your fingers, neck, and chin
Made the bars that fenced me in,
Till Paradise seemed but a wreck
Near your bosom, brow, and neck,
And stars grew wilder, growing wise,
In the splendour of your eyes!
Since the weasel wandered near
Whilst we kissed from ear to ear
And the wet and withered leaves
Blew about your cap and sleeves,
Till the moon sank tired through the ledge
Of the wet and windy hedge?
And we took the starry lane
Back to Dublin town again.

Written 1907–9. Unpublished.

See Appendix A for the history of this poem, and for alternative versions.

In May

IN a nook
That opened south,
You and I
Lay mouth to mouth.

A snowy gull
And sooty daw
Came and looked
With many a caw;

'Such,' I said,
'Are I and you,
When you've kissed me
Black and blue!'

Written 1907. Published, Cuala Edn., 1909.

An early draft is contained in Notebook 33, which includes material of both 1902 and 1907. See Appendix A.

The Quinn Edn. indents alternate lines and has quotation marks at the beginning of all the lines in the last verse.

(*The Masque of May*)

THE chiffchaff and the celandine
The blackbird and the bee
The chestnut branches topped with green
Have met my love and me
And we have played the masque of May
So sweet and commonplace and gay

The sea's first miracle of blue
Bare trees that glitter near the sky
Grow with a love and longing new
Where went my love and I
And there we played the masque of May
So old and infinite and gay.

Completed 4 April 1907. Unpublished. See Appendix A.

The reading 'love' in line 9 is conjectural. The manuscript could read 'line' but this does not make sense.

In Kerry

WE heard the thrushes by the shore and sea,
And saw the golden stars' nativity,
Then round we went the lane by Thomas Flynn,
Across the church where bones lie out and in;
And there I asked beneath a lonely cloud
Of strange delight, with one bird singing loud,
What change you'd wrought in graveyard, rock and
      sea,
This new wild paradise to wake for me. . . .
Yet knew no more than knew these merry sins
Had built this stack of thigh-bones, jaws and shins.

Written 1907–8. Published, Maunsel Edn., 1910.
For a full history of this poem, see Appendix B.

Danny

ONE night a score of Erris men,
A score I'm told and nine,
Said, 'We'll get shut of Danny's noise
Of girls and widows dyin'.

'There's not his like from Binghamstown
To Boyle and Ballycroy,
At playing hell on decent girls,
At beating man and boy.

'He's left two pairs of female twins
Beyond in Killacreest,
And twice in Crossmolina fair
He's struck the parish priest.

'But we'll come round him in the night
A mile beyond the Mullet;
Ten will quench his bloody eyes,
And ten will choke his gullet.'

It wasn't long till Danny came,
From Bangor making way,
And he was damning moon and stars
And whistling grand and gay.

Till in a gap of hazel glen—
And not a hare in sight—
Out lepped the nine-and-twenty lads
Along his left and right.

Then Danny smashed the nose on Byrne,
He split the lips on three,
And bit across the right hand thumb
Of one Red Shawn Magee.

But seven tripped him up behind,
And seven kicked before,
And seven squeezed around his throat
Till Danny kicked no more.

Then some destroyed him with their heels,
Some tramped him in the mud,
Some stole his purse and timber pipe,
And some washed off his blood.

. . .

And when you're walking out the way
From Bangor to Belmullet,
You'll see a flat cross on a stone
Where men choked Danny's gullet.

Written 1907. Published, Maunsel Edn., 1910.

In *John M. Synge: A Few Personal Recollections* (Cuala Press, 1915)
John Masefield described a meeting with Synge in 'May or early
June, 1907'. On page 18 we read:

> 'Presently he told me that he had been writing poetry. He
> handed me a type-written copy of a ballad, and asked me what
> what I thought of it. I told him that I felt the want of an ex-
> planatory stanza near the beginning. "Yes," he said; "But I
> can't take your advice, because then it would not be quite my
> own." He told me the wild picturesque story (of a murder in
> Connaught) which had inspired the ballad.'

An early draft appears in a notebook containing *Vita Vecchia*, which
Synge revised in 1907–8. The above is the accepted text. See Appendix
D for an alternative, and possibly later, version.

The Mergency Man

HE was lodging above in Coom,
And he'd the half of the bailiff's room.

Till a black night came in Coomasaharn
A night of rains you'd swamp a star in.

'To-night,' says he, 'with the devil's weather
The hares itself will quit the heather,

I'll catch my boys with a latch on the door,
And serve my process on near a score.'

The night was black at the fording place
And the flood was up in a whitened race
But devil a bit he'd turn his face,

Then the peelers said, 'Now mind your lepping,
How can you see the stones for stepping?

We'll wash our hands of your bloody job.'
'Wash and welcome,' says he, 'begob.'

He made two leps with a run and dash,
Then the peelers heard a yell and splash.

And the Mergency man in two days and a bit
Was found in the ebb tide stuck in a net.

Written 1908. Published, Maunsel Edn., 1910.

The Maunsel text has been amended in accordance with a corrected typescript in File G.

I've Thirty Months

I'VE thirty months, and that's my pride,
Before my age's a double score,
Though many lively men have died
At twenty-nine or little more.

I've left a long and famous set
Behind some seven years or three,
But there are millions I'd forget
Will have their laugh at passing me.

25, ix, 1908.

Written 1908. Published, Maunsel Edn., 1910.

An alternative version is contained in Notebook 45, and also dated
25.ix.08.

> I've my share of pride
> That I'm near two score
> Though many lively men have died
> On twenty nine or little more
>
> I've passed a famous set
> By seven years or three
> But there are millions I'd forget
> Will crow at passing me.

The text above is that printed in the Maunsel Edn.

On A Birthday

FRIEND of Ronsard, Nashe, and Beaumont,
Lark of Ulster, Meath and Thomond,
Heard from Smyrna and Sahara
To the surf of Connemara,
Lark of April, June, and May,
Sing loudly this my Lady-day.

Written 1908. Published, Cuala Edn., 1909.

One version of this poem was written on the back of one of the leaves
of a late draft of Act III of *Deirdre of the Sorrows*.

(At Coblenz)

OAKS and beeches heath and rushes
You've kept your graces by the Rhine
Since Walter of the Vogelweide
Sang from Coblenz to the Main

But the great-great-great-great bastards
Of the queens that Walter knew
Wear pot-bellies in the breach
And bald heads are potted too

Written 1908, Coblenz. Unpublished.

In the notebook from which this is taken these stanzas are followed
by:

> Oaks and beeches jays and thrushes
> Live as gayly by the Rhine
> Since W. v. d. Wogelweide
> Sang from Coblenz to the Main
>
> But the great-great-great-great bastards
> Of High queens that Walter knew
> Have glasses youth and potted bellies
> And bald heads are potted too

The version of this poem printed in the Greene and Stephens Biography
appears to be a conflation of these two versions, making use of the
first six lines of the second version, and the last two of the first. The
whole has been properly punctuated, and the penultimate line is
given as 'Wear pot-bellies in their breeches'. I have been unable to
find a source for this version. The Stephens manuscript contains only
an exact copy of the notebook versions here given.

(*Abroad*)

SOME go to game, or pray in Rome
I travel for my turning home

For when I've been six months abroad
Faith your kiss would brighten God!

Written 1908, Coblenz. Unpublished.

This poem in Notebook 45 may be a deliberate variation upon a Gaelic original which Frank O'Connor has translated as:

> To go to Rome
> Is little profit, endless pain;
> The Master that you seek in Rome,
> You find at home, or seek in vain.

(From *Kings, Lords, & Commons*, Macmillan 1961.)

Winter

With little money in a great city.

THERE's snow in every street
Where I go up and down,
And there's no woman, man, or dog
That knows me in the town.

I know each shop, and all
These Jews, and Russian Poles,
For I go walking night and noon
To spare my sack of coals.

Written 1896, revised 1907, rewritten 1908. Published, Cuala Edn., 1909.

In a letter to Molly Allgood dated 14 September 1908 Synge enclosed a late draft of this poem, and wrote: 'I got my poem right last night about midnight—when I suppose you were snoring.' Alongside the poem he wrote: 'I wonder if its right after all? Anyhow its better. Be careful of this M.S. and maybe you'll be able to sell it to an American collector for £20 when I'm rotten.' The version in Notebook 45 which was the basis of the text sent in this letter is marked 'A revise of early stuff'. In fact, this poem is a rewritten version of *In the City Again* printed on p. 16 of this edition.

A Question

I ASKED if I got sick and died, would you
With my black funeral go walking too,
If you'd stand close to hear them talk or pray
While I'm let down in that steep bank of clay.

And, No, you said, for if you saw a crew
Of living idiots, pressing round that new
Oak coffin—they alive, I dead beneath
That board,—you'd rave and rend them with your
      teeth.

Written 1908. Published, Cuala Edn., 1909.

In a letter to Molly Allgood dated 10 October 1908 Synge enclosed
a copy of this poem, with the remark: 'I handed over the M.S. of my
poems to Yeats yesterday so I hope that will go alright now. I did
one new poem—that is partly your work—that he says is *Magnificent*.'
      W. B. Yeats wrote in *The Death of Synge* (Cuala Press, 1928): 'I
asked Molly if any words of hers made Synge write "I asked if I got
sick and died" and she said, "He used often to joke about death with
me and one day he said, 'Will you go to my funeral?' and I said,
'No, for I could not bear to see you dead and the others living'"'.'
An early draft of this poem in Notebook 45 is dated 28.9.08.
      The punctuation of the Maunsel version differs slightly from that
of the Cuala Edn. printed here. The Quinn Edn. does not divide
the poem into stanzas, and omits the first comma in the eighth line.

(*A Word on the Life-Force*)

You squirrel angel eel and bat
You seal, sea-serpent water-hen
You badger cur-dog mule and cat
You player with the shapes of men

Written 1908. Unpublished.
From Notebook 47.

(*End of the Book*)

I READ about the Blaskets and Dunquin,
The Wicklow towns and fair days I've been in.
I read of Galway, Mayo, Aranmore,
And men with kelp along a wintry shore.
Then I remembered that that 'I' was I,
And I'd a filthy job—to waste and die.

Written November 1908.

Published in the Greene and Stephens Biography with the omission
of one 'that' in line 5. The following page of Notebook 47, in which
this Poem appears, is dated 23.xi.08.

PART TWO

POETIC DRAMA

The Vernal Play

Synge began writing this play in February 1902 and completed it on 27 March 1902. He revised it later, probably in the autumn of the same year, but ultimately destroyed all but the following two passages. The second passage was probably copied out in the Spring of 1903.

The versions printed here are exact copies of Synge's typescript, save that names have been substituted for initials at those points where Synge did not choose to type out the name of the speaker in full. The stage-directions have been italicized also, and the words 'Scene One' and 'Scene Two' have been added. Early drafts of some passages remain in the notebooks, and the whole play will be discussed in Dr. Saddlemyer's edition of the Plays. An early corrected typescript gives the Dramatis Personae as:

Cermuid
Boinn . . . . his wife
Etan ⎫ . . . two girls
Niave ⎭

Orba ⎫ . . two pipers
Luchtaine ⎭
Old Man

SCENE ONE

Boinn. I hear girls laughing by our morning pool.

Cermuid. Their like come often when May nights are cool
To meet the Glen-Cree shepherds—(*he looks out*)
                                      Two come here
With half a sheaf of garlic, buds of fern
Anemones and blue-bells.

(*Etan and Niave come in behind without seeing the others*)

Etan. Shall we turn
Here east for Glenasmoil?

Niave. The stream is near:
You made great talk this morning of the way
And now you've missed it surely

Etan.   We can lay
Our ferns among the bushes and creep through
This oak-scrub till we find the paths of sheep,
For in this wood, I'm saying, young men sleep
When they're out herding when young lambs are new…

(*They see Boinn & Cermuid*)

Etan. Look there's a mountain woman with her herd.
  They'll know the pathways, find some civil word.

Niave (to Cermuid). I think the rain is ceasing.

Cermuid.   After three
  Or four days with rain falling gods decree
  A soft kind morning on the hills.

Boinn.   The glens
  Are finest then, you'd have a right to go
  South west today, to Clash or Drumnamoe
  To smell the quiet opening of young green
  And purple leaves.

Etan.   We heard a crook't boreen
  Led through these bushes to the Glenasmole,
  And left Bla'claith when the grey cock crew
  To pick these things we've here,—*(showing flowers)*

Niave.   I picked the blue,
  Herself the white and yellow.

Boinn.   Some man stole
  Your word off you you'd come out here today
  But birds and younger women find a way
  To hide their hoping when its love they seek

Cermuid. And yet you've badly chosen for this week
  The shepherds are gone west to Killnahole

Etan. We knew it, shepherd, and came here for peace
  To gather violets and stained hearts-ease,
  Through Glenasmole, And shall we turn here south?

Boinn.   To pass the turning of the glens green mouth
  There is one small wet path.

Niave.   A thick wet cloud
  Is coming now to stir the rivers loud
  And in the shelter of hawthorn tree
  We'll sit a short space with you.

Boinn.   Sycamores
    And larch and birch and sallows breathe new stores
    The time the rain is falling and it warm
    The way it's falling this day.

           (*an old man begins to come in unseen*)—

Cermuid.   After storm
    A light is in these hills turns—(*he stops*) Who comes east?

                (*Old Man comes in*)—

Old Man. By your good leave until the rain has ceased
    I'll shelter with you, if there's a stone or stick
    To let an old man sit.

Boinn.   My cloak is thick
    I'll put an end beneath you. When men grow
    Thus old as you do, with your kind owls-eyes
    And hair like white clouds in a grey sunrise,
    They are as nice as children.
Niave. (*to old man*)   You've come down
    From Glenasmoil?

Old Man.   See how my hood's as brown
    With water as tuft of turfy moss
    Beside two stones in rivers where winds toss
    Their sprays about.

Etan.   Are none left through the glen?
Old Man. There are none old as I.

Boinn.   Nor married men?

Cermuid. (*looking out*) There is a little break behind that ring
    Of cloud, and here two larks begin to sing,
    So patience girls.

Old Man.   Have patience, All that glen
    Is filled with love.

71

Niave.   Your like of bird-eyed men
  Would make it brimful surely.

Old Man.   I'm friend of love
  I think bad of men dying and death bends
  When men make talk of love.

Cermuid. Two rain-bow ends,
  Tilt downward now behind the west above,
  East Killmashogue.

Etan. Who last has come should tell
  Who's in those hills at night.

Old Man. You see a bell
  Of grey touched cloud beyond the low'r glen Du
  That blows to th'east and leaves a tract of blue
  Among the green-tipped beeches?

SCENE TWO

Etan (keening) All young girls must yield to rage
  All firm youth must end in age

Boinn (keening) I call the lambs that browse with fright
  To mourn the man who died tonight

Niave (keening) (*Etan and Orba go out*)
  Every eye must fade and blear
  Every bone bleach bare and clear

Boinn (keening), (*Niave & Luchtain go out*)
  All must rise from earth and clay
  All must end in green decay.
  They are all gone. My verse is hardly ended
  But I will rest a little, for this hour
  I have had pains about me.

Cermuid. With your lips
  You women rhyme the death-rhyme, yet your eyes
  Still say the songs of love

Boinn.   The evening light
   Shines from Glen Cullen and Glen Dhu and the swifts
   Cry with the swallows for the end of day
   No night like this night waking since first we left
   The marsh that ends the sea. From Kilmashogue
   Across Slieve Ruadh all the hills have wrapt
   New blueness from the raining. Hills as these
   Young men in dreams have walked on.

Cermuid.   On the sea
   The long-sailed ships sail from the east and south

Boinn. I see the yellow moth that meets the night
   Before the clouds are red. The air is weighed
   Nor can with all its sweetness wind between
   The boughs where we are standing. Let us climb
   A little higher where the heath is bare
   And while the sun is setting watch the clouds
   That crown the western sea.

Cermuid. I will throw
   My oldest cloak about the old dead body.

   (*When they have pulled the cloak over the body they
                walk up the scene.*)

Boinn. (*breaking down a flowering branch*)
   What fragrance, twist it in my hair that I
   Through all the night may dream of flowery hills

   (*While he crowns her she throws her arms round him*)

   Oh, Man, I would live ever lone with you
   Where every bough and hill turn breathes with joy.

   (*They go out, when they are gone for a little time two
         carrion crows come down and perch on
                the rock above the old man*)

73

The Lady O'Conor

This play was based upon Pat Dirane's story in *The Aran Islands*. It is doubtful whether Synge completed it or not. He certainly planned it and began writing it in 1902. For the original story and Synge's plan for its treatment see Appendix C.

This is the longest remaining fragment of the play. Some lines from it are quoted in the Greene and Stephens Biography. It will be dealt with more fully in Dr. Saddlemyer's edition of the Plays.

SCENE. *Room in castle on cliffs of Clare. Window looking out on the sea and Lady O'Conor at it. O'Conor looking intently at a shrine or sacred picture in the corner.*

Lady C. The fog is down again I cannot see
　　Where the ship vanished (*she at Conor*)
　　　　　　　　　　　　West by Knock-na-lee
　　The waves are louder. Do you hear them Conor?

Conor. I hear them surely (*he comes over*) I'm thinking how
　　poorly God's honour
　　Is slighted here where man's hard set to spare
　　A little thought from these high seas of Clare
　　To think on his soul's weariness and taste
　　The joys that Holy Church lets almost waste
　　Among these wild men here.

Lady C. (*looking eagerly from window*) Was that a cry?

Conor. Some scald crow straying on the northern clift
　　Or lonesome seal this tide has washed adrift
　　　　　　(*He looks out too*)

Lady C. If even birds and fish are lonesome here
　　It's I'm in dread what we'll grow year by year
　　Where scarce a person comes save tinkers only.

Conor. Where God is Lady no soul is truly lonely

74

SCENE. *Capt. & Lady*

Lady C. I'm thinking it's well for you all your life
    Walking the world while I when the wet clouds lift
    Look only all the day on the seas and clift.

Captain. Yet you have silky pillows for your bed
    And golden combs, I'm thinking, comb your head.
    It's roasted hares you'll eat and dearest wine
    And lay your feet on mats of Persian twine
    While we live shut in ships that roll and pitch
    We eating salt till our shin marrows itch
    And drinking filthy water from a barrel
    Our crew half naked through their ripped apparel.

Luasnad, Capa and Laine

This play was begun, like *The Vernal Play*, in February 1902, and completed during the spring. Only fragments of an early draft now remain in Note-book 26. I include here only one fragment for the sake of placing the play upon record and indicating the general tone and manner of its verse. It will be presented more fully in Dr. Saddlemyer's edition of the Plays.

The play is based upon a sentence or two in Geoffrey Keating's *The History of Ireland*, a seventeenth-century book which was reprinted by the Irish Texts Society in 1902. Keating wrote, speaking of the first inhabitants of Ireland, 'Some others say that it is three fishermen who were driven by a storm of wind from Spain unwillingly; and as the island pleased them that they returned for their wives to Spain; and having come back to Ireland again, the deluge was showered upon them at Tuaigh Innbir, so that they were drowned. Capa, Laighne and Luasnad, their names.'

M of Z. Is it hard to die.

Luasnad.   Women know more pain
   When they give birth to children

M of Z.   I am young
   And I have never yet conceived with child—
   Why would the gods who made us now destroy?

Luasnad. The gods have never made us. They have gotten
   Our first grey seed upon the slime of earth
   And have dealt with us as we deal with kine
   Who know the sun (?) brother. We are one
   With all this moon and sea white and the wind
   That slays us. And our passions move when we die
   Among the stars that wander (*2 words illegible*)
   In the great depths of night

M of Z.   Take your hand
   Down from my bosom Luasnad

Luasnad. The great west boulder of our peak has fallen
   And with the next high rising of the tide
   Our death will reach us. There is not any hope.

PART THREE

TRANSLATIONS

I

FROM VILLON, LEOPARDI
AND OTHERS

Prayer of the Old Woman, Villon's Mother

MOTHER of God that's Lady of the Heavens, take myself, the poor sinner, the way I'll be along with them that's chosen.

Let you say to your own Son that He'd have a right to forgive my share of sins, when it's the like He's done, many's the day, with big and famous sinners. I'm a poor aged woman, was never at school, and is no scholar with letters, but I've seen pictures in the chapel with Paradise on one side, and harps and pipes in it, and the place on the other side, where sinners do be boiled in torment; the one gave me great joy, the other a great fright and scaring, let me have the good place, Mother of God, and it's in your faith I'll live always.

It's yourself that bore Jesus, that has no end or death, and He the Lord Almighty, that took our weakness and gave Himself to sorrows, a young and gentle man. It's Himself is our Lord surely, and it's in that faith I'll live always.

Written September 1908. Published, Cuala Edn., 1909.

An Old Woman's Lamentations

THE man I had a love for—a great rascal would kick me in the gutter—is dead thirty years and over it, and it is I am left behind, grey and aged. When I do be minding the good days I had, minding what I was one time, and what it is I'm come to, and when I do look on my own self, poor and dry, and pinched together, it wouldn't be much would set me raging in the streets.

Where is the round forehead I had, and the fine hair, and the two eyebrows, and the eyes with a big gay look out of them would bring folly from a great scholar? Where is my straight shapely nose, and two ears, and my chin with a valley in it, and my lips were red and open?

Where are the pointed shoulders were on me, and the long arms and nice hands to them? Where is my bosom was as white as any, or my straight rounded sides?

It's the way I am this day—my forehead is gone away into furrows, the hair of my head is grey and whitish, my eyebrows are tumbled from me, and my two eyes have died out within my head—those eyes that would be laughing to the men,—my nose has a hook on it, my ears are hanging down, and my lips are sharp and skinny.

That's what's left over from the beauty of a right woman—a bag of bones, and legs the like of two shrivelled sausages going beneath it.

It's of the like of that we old hags do be thinking, of the good times are gone away from us, and we crouching on our hunkers by a little fire of twigs, soon kindled and soon spent, we that were the pick of many.

Written 1908. Published, Cuala Edn., 1909.

The Quinn Edn. has a semicolon instead of a comma and dash in the twentieth line as printed here.

Leopardi

Silvia

ARE you bearing in mind that time when there was a fine look out of your eyes, and yourself, pleased and thoughtful, were going up the boundaries that are set to childhood? That time the quiet rooms, and the lanes about the house, would be noisy with your songs that were never tired out; the time you'd be sitting down with some work that is right for women, and well pleased with the hazy coming times you were looking out at in your own mind.

May was sweet that year, and it was pleasantly you'd pass the day.

Then I'd leave my pleasant studies, and the paper I had smudged with ink where I would be spending the better part of the day, and cock my ears from the sill of my father's house, till I'd hear the sound of your voice, or of your loom when your hands moved quickly. It's then I would set store on the quiet sky and the lanes and little places, and the sea was far away in one place and the high hills in another.

There is no tongue will tell till the judgment what I feel in myself those times.

Written 1908. Published, Maunsel Edn., 1910.

Colin Muset, an old poet,
complains to his patron (I)

From the old French

I'M getting old in your big house, and you've never stretched your hand with a bit of gold to me, or a day's wages itself. By my faith in Mary, it's not that way I'll serve you always, living on my pocket, with a few coppers only, and a small weight in my bag. You've had me to this day, singing on your stairs before you, but I'm getting a good mind to be going off, when I see my purse flattened out, and my wife does be making a fool of me from the edge of the door.

It's another story I hear when I come home at night and herself looks behind me, and sets her eye on my bag stuffed to bursting, and I maybe with a grey, decent coat on my back. It's that time she's not long leaving down her spinning and coming with a smile, ready to choke me with her two hands squeezing my neck. It's then my sons have a great rage to be rubbing the sweat from my horse, and my daughter isn't long wringing the necks on a pair of chickens, and making a stew in the pot. It's that day my youngest will bring me a towel, and she with nice manners. . . . It's a full purse, I tell you, makes a man lord in his own house.

Written 1908. Published, Cuala Edn., 1909.

An old poet, Colin Muset,
complains to his patron (II)

(After the old French)

I'M growing old with singing on your stairs,
And I more starving than your dogs or mares,
Yet, by my faith in Mary, I'll not stay,
I'll go to better men, or get my pay.
There's gallous times when I go home at eight,
And there's my wife to curse me at the gate.
But when she looks behind my back and sees
A bursting budget, then there's joy and ease;
It's then my sons have rage to rub the sweat
From my old mare, and soon the tea is wet
By Mary-Bridget, then she makes a stew
Of two young cocks, and there's my youngest too
Brings me my little towel in her hand,
With lovely manners . . . Faith we're mighty grand.
And then I count my gains, as it is proper.
If you'd be lord at home show gold and copper.

Written 1908. Published, Dolmen Edn., 1961.

It is not certain that the last two lines of this poem are completely Synge's.
The MS. alteration of Synge's draft does not appear to be in his hand. Synge's
own corrected typescript runs:

    when   *gains*   *herself is honey*
And then I count my pieces, for its funny
IF YOU'D BE LORD IN YOUR OWN HOUSE SHOW MONEY.

Walter Von Der Vogelweide

I NEVER set my two eyes on a head was so fine as your head, but I'd no way to be looking down into your heart.

It's for that I was tricked out and out—that was the thanks I got for being so steady in my love.

I tell you, if I could have laid my hands on the whole set of the stars, the moon and the sun along with it, by Christ I'd have given the lot to her. No place have I set eyes on the like of her, she's bad to her friends, and gay and playful to those she'd have a right to hate. I ask you can that behaviour have a good end come to it?

Written 1908. Published, Maunsel Edn., 1910.

Judaslied 14th Century

OH our poor Judas, what is it you've done, to have sold
your Lord God? It's for that you'll have the pains of
Hell, and will be ever and always keeping company with
Lucifer Oh Lord God!

Written 1908, Coblenz. Published, Dolmen Edn., 1961.
From Notebook 49.

II

PETRARCH

SONNETS FROM 'LAURA IN DEATH'

These translations were made in 1907, largely as experiments. The titles
of those published in the Cuala Edition were provided by Synge. It seems
likely that those printed first in the Maunsel Edition were given titles by
another hand. I have not imitated these titles in publishing the five addi-
tional sonnets in this edition but have left them with the headings Synge
gave them on his own typescripts.

Laura being dead, Petrarch finds trouble in all the things of the earth

LIFE is flying from me, not stopping an hour, and Death is
making great strides following my track. The days about
me, and the days passed over me are bringing me desola-
tion, and the days to come will be the same surely.

All things that I am bearing in mind, and all things I am
in dread of, are keeping me in troubles, in this way one
time, in that way another time, so that if I wasn't taking
pity on my own self it's long ago I'd have given up my
life.

If my dark heart has any sweet thing it is turned away
from me, and then farther off I see the great winds where
I must be sailing. I see my good luck far away in the har-
bour, but my steersman is tired out, and the masts and the
ropes on them are broken, and the beautiful lights where
I would be always looking are quenched.

Published, Cuala Edn., 1909.

He asks his heart to raise itself up to God

WHAT is it you're thinking, lonesome heart? For what is it you're turning back ever and always to times that are gone away from you? For what is it you're throwing sticks on the fire where it is your own self that is burning?

The little looks and sweet words you've taken one by one and written down among your songs, are gone up into the Heavens, and it's late you know well, to go seeking them on the face of the earth.

Let you not be giving new life every day to your own destruction, and following a fool's thoughts forever. Let you seek Heaven when there is nothing left pleasing on the earth, and it a poor thing if a great beauty, the like of her, would be destroying your peace and she living or dead.

Published, Cuala Edn., 1909.

He wishes he might die and follow Laura

In the years of her age the most beautiful and the most flowery,—the time Love has his mastery—Laura, who was my life, has gone away leaving the earth stripped and desolate. She has gone up into the Heavens, living and beautiful and naked, and from that place she is keeping her Lordship and her rein upon me, and I crying out, Ohone, when will I see that day breaking that will be my first day with herself in Paradise?

My thoughts are going after her, and it is that way my soul would follow her, lightly, and airily, and happily, and I would be rid of all my great troubles. But what is delaying me is the proper thing to lose me utterly, to make me a greater weight on my own self.

Oh, what a sweet death I might have died this day three years to-day!

Published, Cuala Edn., 1909.
The Quinn Edn. omits the first comma in the second line as printed here.

Laura is ever present to him

IF the birds are making lamentation, or the green banks are moved by a little wind of summer, or you can hear the waters making a stir by the shores that are green and flowery.

That's where I do be stretched out thinking of love, writing my songs, and herself that Heaven shows me though hidden in the earth I set my eyes on, and hear the way that she feels my sighs and makes an answer to me.

'Alas,' I hear her say, 'why are you using yourself up before the time is come, and pouring out a stream of tears so sad and doleful.

'You'd do right to be glad rather, for in dying I won days that have no ending, and when you saw me shutting up my eyes I was opening them on the light that is eternal.'

Published, Maunsel Edn., 1910.
Synge originally headed this draft 'Sonnet. 11'.

He ceases to speak of her graces and her virtues which are no more

THE eyes that I would be talking of so warmly, and the arms, and the hands, and the feet, and the face, that are after calling me away from myself and making me a lonesome man among all people.

The hair that was of shining gold, and brightness of the smile that was the like of an angel's surely, and was making a paradise of this earth, are turned to a little dust, that knows nothing at all.

And yet I myself am living; it is for this I am making a complaint to be left without the light I had such a great love for, in good fortune and bad, and this will be the end of my songs of love, for the vein where I had cleverness is dried up, and everything I have is turned to complaint only.

Published, Maunsel Edn., 1910.

Synge originally headed this draft 'Sonnet 24'. The Maunsel Edn. has 'the earth' instead of 'this earth' in the seventh line; I have followed the manuscript.

He is jealous of the Heavens and the earth

WHAT a grudge I am bearing the earth that has its arms about her, and is holding that face away from me, where I was finding peace from great sadness.

What a grudge I am bearing the Heavens that are after taking her, and shutting her in with greediness, the Heavens that do push their bolt against so many.

What a grudge I am bearing the blessed saints that have got her sweet company, that I am always seeking; and what a grudge I am bearing against Death, that is standing in her two eyes, and will not call me with a word.

Published, Cuala Edn., 1909.

The fine time of the year
increases Petrarch's sorrow

THE south wind is coming back, bringing the fine season, and the flowers, and the grass, her sweet family, along with her. The swallow and the nightingale are making a stir, and the spring is turning white and red in every place.

There is a cheerful look on the meadows, and peace in the sky, and the sun is well pleased, I'm thinking, looking downward, and the air and the waters and the earth herself are full of love, and every beast is turning back looking for its mate.

And what is coming to me is great sighing and trouble, which herself is drawing out of my deep heart, herself that has taken the key of it up to Heaven.

And it is this way I am, that the singing birds, and the flowers of the earth, and the sweet ladies, with their grace and comeliness, are the like of a desert to me, and wild beasts astray in it.

Published, Cuala Edn., 1909.

He understands the great cruelty of Death

My flowery and green age was passing away, and I feeling a chill in the fires had been wasting my heart, for I was drawing near the hillside above the grave.

Then my sweet enemy was making a start, little by little, to give over her great wariness, the way she was wringing a sweet thing out of my sharp sorrow. The time was coming when Love and Decency can keep company, and Lovers may sit together and say out all things are in their hearts. But Death had his grudge against me, and he got up in the way, like an armed robber, with a pike in his hand.

Published, Cuala Edn., 1909.

The sight of Laura's house reminds him
of the great happiness he has lost

Is this the nest in which my Phœnix put on her feathers of gold and purple, my Phœnix that did hold me under her wing, and she drawing out sweet words and sighs from me? Oh, root of my sweet misery, where is that beautiful face, where light would be shining out, the face that did keep my heart like a flame burning? She was without a match upon the earth, I hear them say, and now she is happy in the Heavens.

And she has left me after her dejected and lonesome, turning back all times to the place I do be making much of for her sake only, and I seeing the light on the little hills where she took her last flight up into the Heavens, and where one time her eyes would make sunshine and it night itself.

Published, Cuala Edn., 1909.

He sends his rhymes to the tomb of Laura
to pray her to call him to her

LET you down, sorrowful rhymes, to the rock is covering my dear treasure, and then let you call out till herself that is in the Heavens will make answer, though her dead body is lying in a shady place.

Let you say to her that it is tired out I am with being alive, with steering in bad seas, but I am going after her step by step, gathering up what she let fall behind her.

It is of her only I do be thinking, and she living and dead, and now I have made her with my songs so that the whole world may know her, and give her the love that is her due.

May it please her to be ready for my own passage that is getting near, may she be there to meet me, herself in the Heavens, that she may call me, and draw me after her.

Published, Maunsel Edn., 1910.

Synge's original heading was 'Sonnet 59'. The Maunsel Edn. has 'hard rock' in the first line, but I can find no other authority for this reading.

Only he who mourns her and Heaven that possesses her knew her while she lived

Ah, Death, it is you that have left the world cold and shady, with no sun over it. It's you have left Love without eyes or arms to him, you've left liveliness stripped, and beauty without a shape to her, and all courtesy in chains, and honesty thrown down into a hole. I am making lamentation alone, though it isn't myself only has a cause to [be] crying out. Since you, Death, have crushed the first seed of goodness in the whole world, and with it gone what place will we find a second?

The air and the earth and seas would have a good right to be crying out, and they pitying the race of men that is left without herself, like a meadow without flowers or a ring robbed of jewellery.

The world didn't know her the time she was in it, but I myself knew her, and I left now to be weeping in this place; and the Heavens knew her, the Heavens that are giving an ear this day to my crying out.

Published, Maunsel Edn., 1910.
Synge originally headed this '66'.
The Maunsel Edn. differs in some respects from the manuscript version printed here.

Laura waits for him in Heaven

THE first day she passed up and down through the Heavens, gentle and simple were left standing, and they in great wonder, saying one to the other:—

'What new light is that? What new beauty at all? The like of herself hasn't risen up these long years from the common world.'

And herself, well pleased with the Heavens, was going forward, matching herself with the most perfect that were before her, yet one time, and another, waiting a little, and turning her head back to see if myself was coming after her. It's for that I'm lifting up all my thoughts and will into the Heavens, because I do hear her praying that I should be making haste forever.

Published, Cuala Edn., 1909.

The Quinn Edn. omits the dash at the close of the first paragraph.

Sonnet 12

I WAS never anyplace where I saw so clearly one I do be wishing to see when I do not see, never in a place where I had the like of this freedom in my self, and where the light of loving making was strong in the sky. I never saw any valley with so many spots in it where a man is quiet and peaceful, and I wouldn't think that Love himself in Cyprus had a nest so nice and curious. The waters are holding their discourse on love, and the wind with them and the branches, and fish, and the flowers and the grass, the lot of them are giving hints to me that I should love forever.

But yourself are calling to me out of Heaven to pray me by the memory of the bitter death that took you from me that I should put small store on the world or on the tricks are in it.

Published, Dolmen Edn., 1961

The original reads 'Cypress', which is incorrect, and has been altered as the mistake was clearly one of spelling rather than translation. The title in the Dolmen Edn. was given as 'He considers that he should set little store on earthly beauty'.

Sonnet 13

How many times, running away from all people and from myself if I was able, I go out to my little nook, with my two eyes crying tears on my breast and on the grass under me, and breaking the air with the great sighs I do be giving.

How many times, and I heavy with sorrow, I have stretched out in shady places and woods, seeking always in my thoughts for herself that death has taken from me, and calling out to her one time and again that she might come near me. Then in some form of a high goddess I see her rising up out of the clearest pool of the Sorga, my sweet river, and putting herself to sit upon the bank.

Or other days I have seen her on the fresh grass and she picking flowers like a living lady, yet showing me in her look she has a pity for myself.

Published, Dolmen Edn., 1961.
The title given in the Dolmen Edn. was 'He recalls his visions of her'.

Sonnet 14

Sᴡᴇᴇᴛ spirit you that do be coming down so often to put a sweetness on my sad night-time with a look from those eyes death has not quenched, but made more deep and beautiful:

How much it is a joy to me that you throw a light on my dark days, so that I am beginning to find your beauty in the places where I did see you often.

Where I did go long years, and I singing of yourself, I go now, making lamentations for my own sharp sorrows.

It is when I have great sorrow only that I find rest, for it is then when I turn round I see and know you, by your walk and your voice, and your face, and the cloak round you.

Published, Dolmen Edn., 1961.

The title in the Dolmen Edn. was given as 'He finds comfort and rest in his sorrows'.

Sonnet 25

If I had thought that the voice of my grief would have a value I would have made a greater number surely of my first sorrow and in a finer manner:

But she who made me speak them out and who stood in the summit of my thoughts is dead at this time, and I am not able to make these rough verses sweet or clear.

And in surety those times all I was wishing was to ease my sad heart in any way I was able and not to gain an honour for myself, and it was weep I was seeking and not the honour men might win of it, and now it is the one pleasure I am seeking that she would call to me and I silent and tired out.

Published, Dolmen Edn., 1961.
The title given in the Dolmen Edn. was 'He considers the reasons for his verses'.

Sonnet 72

THERE was one time maybe when it was a sweet thing to love—though I would be hard set to say when it was—but now it is a bitter thing and there is nothing bitterer. The man who is teaching a truth should know it better than any other, and that is the way I am with my great sorrow.

Herself that was the honour of our age, [and] now is in the heavens where all cherish her, made my [times of ease] in her days short and rare, and now she has taken all rest from me.

Cruel Death has taken every good thing from me, and from this out no good luck could make up for the loss of that beautiful spirit that is set free.

I used to be weeping and making songs, and I dont know at this day what way I'd turn a verse, but day and night the sorrow that is banked up in my heart breaks out on my tongue and through my eyes.

Published, Dolmen Edn., 1961.

The words in brackets have been added by the editor, in the first case to improve the syntax and clarify the sense, and in the second case to fill a gap left in Synge's typescript. The title given in the Dolmen Edn. was 'Petrarch is unable to contain his grief'.

APPENDIX A

WORKSHEETS OF 'IS IT A MONTH'

(a) In Notebook 33 there are ten pages of draft verse which all appear to have been written over a short period. These drafts clearly resulted in the completion of the three poems, 'Is it a Month', 'In May', and 'The Masque of May'. Although some pages contain nothing at all of 'Is it a Month' I print all the pages here as other pages clearly show that all three poems were, in their early stages, involved in each other. It is not possible to determine the order in which the pages were written. It seems as if the first page is the latest, but it is not clear that the last page in the series was written first, or that the last, the penultimate, and the antepenultimate were written in that order. I therefore print the pages in the order in which they are set out in the notebook.

I

4/iv/07

The chiff chaff and the celandine
  The blackbird and the bee
The chesnut branches topped with green
  Have met my love and me
And we have played the masque of May
    sweet
So old and commonplace and gay

                    glitter near
The seas first miracle of blue
  Bare trees that   the sky
Shone with a love and longing new
  Where went my love and I
And there we played the masque of May
  So old and infinite and gay

(2)

The chiffchaff, swallow, humble bee
Are met ~~today~~ in happy company
With the linnet robin and the wren

And a sight of girls and men
For
To play the merry masque of May
Every actor still would play
                    blue and
And the sea's a   jewelled plate
                this
And the elms are reared elate

(3)

We went between the rocks and sea
   The little path from Bray

We went the path that runs between
   The sea and hill from Bray

And the hill was gold and green
   The sea like silver lay

And on the slope against the south
   The air grew warm and sweet

And there we lay warm mouth to mouth
   With cowslips to our feet

And snowy gulls and sooty daws
   Played round above the glen
   Played with the

Like [illeg.] wild [illeg.]
   [illeg.] me and you

(4)

                    With us today
                Mays masque and play
The   and celandine
                        thrush and
The blackbird and the | bee
The birches touched with green
Have met my love and me
And staged the masque of May
All lovers like to play

The linnet, and the wren
The cowslip and the rose
The furse that's in the glen
The fly upon the sloes
            staged with us
Have brought on stage today
The masque all lovers play

104

(5)

We prised our finger tip
Our   our double
Our red and happy lips
Among our kith and kin
All things that ~~waken~~ love to play
The Lovers masque of May

Mays Masque that lovers play

That stage and sing the Masque of May
Spite of all that Bishops say

(6)

Is it a month since I and you
Watched the stars above Glen Dubh
*   stars rising round*
Till Paradise seemed but a wreck
Near this little ear and neck

And the then and   hedge
Nettles [illeg.] along its edge

Stars met their glitter in your eyes
And grew more golden growing wise

With them we've staged for May
the merry Masque of spring
That spite of Bishops Nay
wise lovers ~~to~~ love to sing

(7)

*   staged today*
With them ~~with~~ we ~~set the play~~
The lovers Masque of May
That 'spite of Bishop's 'Nay'
All lovers love to sing

*   of love and spring*
*   set*
With them weve ~~seen~~ | today
Mays Masque upon the stage
That 'spite of Bishop's 'Nay'
Is joy to every age
Is the life of every [illeg.]

105

All lovers love to sing
Wise

(8)

The loghing lark and wren
The half awakened rose
The woodcock in the glen
The fly upon the sloes

The silly dream; Rose
    red mad
        soft
My sweet | bee-ridden rose
    sly
~~The~~   woodcock in the glen

          we'll   with these
With them ~~we~~ | set | today
The.
~~Masque May's~~ Masque upon the stage
That spite of Bishop's Nay
Is sung by sot and sage

(9)

~~The~~ Till near this bosom brow and neck
Paradise seemed but a wreck
Stars that glittered in your eyes
Grew more golden growing wise

Stars grew golden growing wise
In the glitter of your eyes.

(10)

White gulls and hasty cackling daws
    Two worlds of blue
      ~~wit and~~
Such the silly   ~~town~~ laws
    Dividing me and you

On a Monday morn in May
  We took the little path from Bray
To a nook that faced the south
Where we lay with mouth to mouth,

106

There the sun
A white gull and a lucky daw
Then along the hill we saw

A snowy sea gull and a daw
Flying round the tids of
(Such' I said are 'I and you)

(*b*) From a letter to Molly Allgood dated 14 May 1907 (from a transcript in the Stephens MS).

Is it a month or a year's pain since I
Watched with my chosen how red twilights die
When her soft fingers, neck, soft arms and chin,
And her young voice, tempered to twilight's key
Brought back my spirit's lost liberty
Till the stars vault, half-shrinking seemed to crush
Our boundless joy, who went in lanes of slush
Kissing from ear to ear, from throat to brow
Losing the past and present in one radiant now
Till we went silent to the spattered train
That led us to the city, and mere life again.

(*c*) A typescript altered in manuscript and then completely crossed out (from a file marked 'Reserved Poems (Duplicates) 1906–1908 and Earlier').

Hare and weazel wandered by
While we kissed on lip and eye

Rat and rabbit wandered near
While we kissed from ear-to ear   throat

Beneath a larch and hazel bough
We kissed from ear and throat to brow,
While your fingers, hair, and chin
Made the bars that fenced me in,
Till Paradise seemed but a wreck
Near your bosom brow and neck,
And stars grew wilder growing wise
In the ~~spend~~ splendour of your eyes.

Though ~~we rose~~ [illeg.]
Then the wet and withered leaves
Blew about your cap and sleeves,
And the moon sank tired through the ledge
Of the wet and windy hedge

Till   ~~Then we took the starry lane~~
        ~~To the morning's world again.~~

107

~~Clarmorris back again~~

stony

~~Till we took the narrow track~~
~~From Lough Ouler leading back~~

(*d*) On the other side of version (*c*) above, in manuscript.

Where hare and weazel wandered by
Long we kissed on lip and eye
While your fingers neck and chin
Made the bars that fenced me in
Till the wet and withered leaves
Blew about your cap and sleeves
And still grew wilder growing wise
In the ~~*splendour*~~ *of your eyes*
stillness

(*e*) One of three fair typescripts in an envelope. These copies may not be by Synge.

Where hare and weazel wandered by
Long we kissed on lip and eye,
brow
While your fingers ~~neck~~ and chin,
Made the bars that faced me in.
And
~~Till~~ the wet and withered leaves
Blew about your cap and sleeves.
Till Paradise seemed but a wreck
Near your bosom, brow and neck,
And stars grew wilder, growing wise,
In the ~~splendour~~ of your eyes.
stillness

Till Paradise seemed but a wreck
Near the ~~*splendour*~~ *of your neck*
glory

(*f*) A typescript differing from version (*e*) above only in reading 'While your fingers neck and chin' and 'In the laughter of your eyes' (from a file marked 'Poems for Maunsel's Edition').

(*g*) Corrected typescript, with some lines also in manuscript alongside (from a file marked 'F. Poems by J. M. Synge'. There is a note in this file in Yeats's hand stating that this file contains earlier versions of poems in the Cuala Press Edition).

Is it a month since I and you
Watched stars rising from Glen Dubh,
Underneath
~~Since beneath~~ that hazel bough
Long we kissed from throat to brow,
Since your fingers, neck, and chin
Made the bars that fenced me in,
~~While your voice in twilight's key~~
~~Wrought my spirit's ecstasy~~
Till Paradise seemed but a wreck
Near your bosom, brow, and neck,
        wilder
And stars grew older, growing wise,
In the splendour of your eyes!

        brow
Since we kissed from ~~ear~~ to ear
~~While~~
Till ~~Till~~ the weazels wandered near,
And the wet and withered leaves
Blew about your cap and sleeves,
Till
~~And~~ the moon sank tired through the ledge
Of the wet and windy hedge?
        starry
~~And we took the slushy lane~~
           stet.

~~Back to Dublin town again.~~

Is it a month since I and you
In the moon and starlight of star and moon
In the starlight of Glen Dubh
Stretched beneath a hazel bough
Kissed from ear and throat to brow,
Since etc.
Since the weazel wandered near
Whilst we kissed from ear to ear

These manuscripts led me to believe that version (*g*) was as near
to a final version as Synge got. Unfortunately for my theory,
however, there is a passage in the Stephens MS. which reads:

'I found a sheet of paper on which John had written—"Poems for Maunsel's
edition of my verse to be added—with one or two possible exceptions to
those now being printed by Miss Yeats. J.M.S. Jan. 8. 1909". The words

"consult Mr. W. B. Yeats" were in brackets and probably written later. To the sheet there remained attached three poems: "In Kerry", "The Curse", and an unnamed poem beginning "Where hare and weazle wandered by." '

It is not safe to assume that this version is the one listed here under (d), or even either of the ones listed as (e) and (f). It seems, however, that the version in the body of this book was rejected by Synge in favour of a shorter version, most probably (but not certainly) similar to (d). Nevertheless it seems to me that (d), (e), and (f) seem fragmentary in a way that (g) does not. I have therefore chosen to make use of (g) as if it were the final version, believing that taking this editorial liberty has led to the inclusion in the canon of a better poem than the one Synge apparently chose himself.

APPENDIX B

THE WORKSHEETS OF 'IN KERRY'

In Kerry' presents more clearly than any other poem Synge's method of working. In publishing transcripts of his worksheets I have taken only one liberty with the texts: where Synge has made manuscript corrections vertically up the margin of the page rather than horizontally, I have placed these at the bottom of my transcript, and not attempted to imitate too precisely the actual layout of the manuscript. Typescript is indicated here by ordinary printing, and manuscript by italics. Where Synge has indicated that some material he has crossed out ought to remain, I have inserted the word 'stet', whether or not Synge used this particular method of indicating his judgment. I have made no attempt to correct punctuation or spelling errors. As has already been pointed out, it is almost impossible to date many of Synge's manuscripts. In the case of this particular poem it is only possible to date one version with any accuracy. The order in which the versions are printed, therefore, simply expresses my own view of the chronology of the various drafts, working almost entirely from internal evidence.

There are two passages in the Stephens MS. which bear upon the composition of this poem. Writing of a trip he made with his father in the late summer of 1908, Edward Stephens said:

'After breakfast my father and I went to see the ruined Abbey in Lord Ardilaun's demesne, of which the gate opened into the village. The remains of the Abbey had suffered terribly from delapidation and later from vulgar restoration. I took some photographs of its doorways and then, as we were wandering through the long grass, we looked in through a window opening and saw a stack of human bones piled 4ft. high against a wall. Never before had I seen so strange a result of the belief that bones found in a grave yard should not be reinterred. It was such a pile that John had in mind when he wrote of the insolvable problem of love—

"Yet knew no more than knew those merry sins
Had built this stack of thigh bones, jaws and shins."

Aunt Lizzie had told me that, when she was a girl, there was a much larger stack of bones in Cong Abbey, but someone had sent a boat from Galway to take them for bone manure. The cargo was loaded, so the story ran, but it never reached Galway, for an old woman went down on her knees and cursed the boat as it set sail, and it sank in Lough Corrib and was never heard of again.'

A few pages later Edward Stephens writes of telling this anecdote to J. M. Synge. He says of Synge's reactions:

'He was interested in my impressions of Cong Abbey too and in my seeing bones stacked up against its walls. The significance of the remains of the unnamed dead always impressed his mind.'

It is not impossible, therefore, that the later drafts of 'In Kerry' were written after this time, for it may well have been Edward Stephens's anecdote that provided Synge with the final lines.

I

A corrected typescript from the file marked 'Biographical Matter only not to be printed as literary work'.

We came behind the rain from Murphy's inn
And saw the splendour of the night begin
                              and to draw
To redden on the mountains, ma~~king~~ near
                              then
The vallies of Glen Cullen, growing clear
Behind bare sycamores that in the west
                    nun's lace to your
Clung to the sky like ~~lace about the~~ breast
With fine textures
Of women richly dressed.

                         shining
We heard the thrushes by the silver sea
And saw the ~~golden~~ stars nativity,
Then   were wrapped
~~And~~ we ~~seemed lost~~ within a lonely cloud
Of strange delight, where birds were singing loud,
The rest was Silence: with the fragrant smells
                              Lady buds
Of opening furze and grass, and ~~saps~~ that swell!
~~Each flower's honey well.~~
And then I asked why with your lips to mine
Had
~~Have~~ all these wonders added eight or nine
New volumes to their glory? Were stars made new,
Because your little lips were round and true?

112

> *now you'd transfigured earth and sea*
I asked ~~what you had laid on earth and sea~~
This more than   to
That an unearthly Paradise ~~should~~wake for me?
>   *'d   callous*
With what new gold ~~had~~ you ~~en~~cased the moon?
>   *what   s*
With new anthem raised the ~~raver~~ river's tune?
And why did every sound with rapture break
While my two lips were on your honied cheek?

II

Transcript, from the Stephens MS., of a letter from Synge to Molly Allgood dated 16.5.07. Synge refers to quoting these verses on 'our wet walk', which was probably a walk along the lane from the Glencullen road by Killigar to the Scalp.

> We came behind the rain from Murphy's inn
> And saw the splendour of the night begin
> Behind bare sycamores, that in the west
> Clung to the sky like lace about the breast
>   Of Woman richly dressed.
>
> We heard the thrushes by the shore and sea
> And saw the golden stars nativity
> Then in the furze we met a lonely cloud
> Of strange delight, where birds were singing loud
> The rest was silence, with the smell
> Of golden honey in its golden well.
>
> And then I asked why with your lips to mine
> Had all these glories added eight or nine
> New volumes to their glory? Were stars made new
> Because your little lips were round and true?
> I asked what change you'd wrought in land and sea
> This more than earthly Paradise to wake for me?
> With what new gold you'd cased the moon,
> With what new anthems raised the rivers' tune?
> And why did every sound with rapture break
> While my two lips were on your honied cheek?

III

From a file marked 'G'.

We heard the thrushes by the shore and sea,
And saw the golden stars nativity,

And then I asked beneath

~~Then in the furze we met~~ a lonely cloud,
Of strange delight, with one bird singing loud,
~~The rest was silence with the smell~~   *short*
~~Of honey in its golden well.~~

then   was every

And then I asked were all the stars made new,

its

Because their shining bent and met with you,
~~I asked~~ What change you'd wrought in/land and sea,   *all this*
This ~~more than~~ earthly paradise to wake for me,   *night of   long*
With what new/gold you'd cased the/moon,   ~~happy~~ *happy –short*
With what new anthems raised the rivers tune,
And why my lips that round your lips delayed
Trembled like priests of ~~God's high thought~~ afraid. *their ~~high~~ faith*
                                                    own

IV

A loose typescript from file 'G'.

We heard the thrushes by the shore and sea,
And saw the golden stars nativity,

I asked

And then, beneath a ~~soft and~~ lonely cloud
Of strange delight, with one bird singing loud,

W   in all the

~~I asked~~ what change you'd wrought in land and sea
This night of paradise to wake for me,

gilt   stars and

With *what* new gold you'd ~~cased~~ the ~~callous~~ moon

singing

With what new ~~anthem~~ raised the river's tune,

ed

~~With what new honey touch the furze and grass~~

sent–   s to

With what new sweetness made the south wind pass
And still I asked till by the shore and sea
The thrushes sang the day's nativity
And still I question till the shore and sea
Heard thrushes sing the day's nativity

114

V

From a file marked 'G', written on the back of another manuscript.

With what new gold you'd gilt the stars and moon
With what new silence filled this lonely Dun

VI

From the file marked 'Biographical Matter Only'.

In Kerry
We heard the thrushes by the shore and sea,
And saw the golden stars nativity,
And then I asked beneath a lonely cloud,
Of strange delight, with one bird singing loud,
What change you'd wrought in all the land and sea
This new wild paradise to wake for me,
With what new gold you'd gilt the stars and moon,
                    breath you'd
With what new ~~shadows~~ filled our rocky Dun,
And still I asked till by the shore and sea
The thrushes sang the day's nativity.

~~With what new breathing filled this rocky Dun~~
~~With what new life made wild this rocky Dun~~
                    dream   bright
                    gleam
With what new silver faced this rocky Dun

                              to go in with the Love Lyrics

VII

From Notebook 45. The poem on the opposite page is dated
28.9.08.

We heard the thrushes by the shore and sea
And saw the golden stars nativity
Then in the furze ~~beneath~~ we met a lonely cloud
Of strange delight, with one bird singing loud
I asked what change you'd wrought in land and sea
This ~~glade of~~ earthly paradise to make for me
With what new gold you'd cased the happy moon
With what new anthem raised the rivers tune
And why my lips that round your wrist delayed
Trembled like priests of their own faith afraid

115

VIII

From a file marked 'Reserved Poems (Duplicates) 1906–1908 and Earlier'.

We heard the thrushes by the shore and sea
And saw the golden stars nativity,
Then in the furze we met a lonely cloud
     with one bird
Of strange delight, ~~where~~ birds were singing loud,
The rest was silence with the smell
Of honey in its golden well.

And then I asked were all the stars made new
    shining
Because their ~~brightness~~ bent and met with you,
I asked what change you'd wrought in land and sea,
This more than earthly paradise to wake for me,
With what new gold you'd cased the moon,
With what new anthems raised the rivers tune
~~And why my lips that played about your wrist~~
~~Trembled like nuns by some brute robber kissed.~~

    round your wrist delayed
and why my lips that played about your wrist
    touched you (half afraid)—
~~*Trembled like eyes*~~ *in some high visions mist*
      crown
    by God's high thought dismayed

IX

From a file marked 'G'.

   white tingla songs
We came/ where ~~many~~ bones are seen
Around the little church of ~~Michenleen~~
   the chapel's called Saint Michauleen

We heard the thrushes by the shore and sea
And saw the golden stars nativity
And then I asked, beneath a lonely cloud
Of strange delight, with one bird singing loud,

116

What change you'd wrought in all the land and sea
This earthly paradise to wake for me,
With what new ~~happy~~ gold you'd ~~eased~~ the moon,   gilded all
With what new anthem raised the river's tune,
With what new honey touched the furze and grass
And With what ~~new~~ sweetness sent the winds to pass.
                                by
And still I wondered till ~~the~~ shore and sea
The thrushes sang the day's nativity.

We heard the thrushes by the shore and sea
And saw the golden stars nativity
And then I asked beneath a lonely cloud
Of strange delight with one bird singing loud
What change you'd made with jawbones, ribs and thighs
Yet rotting bones seemed merry white and wise
And little tomb-stones shone so white an free
A night's wild paradise awoke for me

What change you'd made with jaw-bones ribs and thighs
To make this ground a strip of Paradise.

X

From Notebook 45, facing XI.

    We heard the thrushes by the shore and sea

    We heard the thrushes on a church'es mound
    Where many bones
        mens white brittle bone are laid around
    And then I asked beneath a lonely cloud
    Of strange delight with one bird singing loud
    ~~*with what*~~
    What change you'd wrought in all the land and sea
    With what new laughter touch this   [illeg.]
    With what new gold you'd gilded all the moon
    With what rare anthem raised the rivers tune
        what new singing

    Where bees fetch honey for their swarming cribs
    And we're two skulls and backs and forty ribs.

XI

From Notebook 45, facing X.

    We heard the thrushes in a churches' ground
    Where grey and brittle bones were laid around

117

And then I asked beneath a low white cloud
Of strange delight, with one bird singing loud
What change you'd wrought in all the land and sea
With what new whiteness touched these men's debris
With what new gold you'd gilded all the moon
With what new singing raised the rivers tune

XII

From a file marked 'G'.

> We heard the thrushes by the shore and sea,
> And saw the golden stars nativity
> And then
> I asked, this night, beneath a lonely cloud
> Of strange delight, with one bird singing loud,
> What change you'd wrought in all the land and sea
> This new cold paradise to wake for me,
> With what new gold you'd gilt the stars and moon,
> To what new treble set the river's tune.
>
> But when we came across the little site
> Of Michael's Church where bones lie free and white,
> I asked what paradise, what merry sins
> Had left this little stack of jaws and shins.

XIII

A fair typescript on the back of XII.

> We heard the thrushes by the shore and sea,
> And saw the golden stars nativity
> And then I asked beneath a lonely cloud
> Of strange delight, with one bird singing loud,
> What change you'd wrought in all this land and sea,
> This new cold paradise to wake for me,
> With what new time you'd stirred the rivers tune
> With what new gold you'd gilt the stars and moon . . .
>
> But when we reached the high and stony site
> Of Michael's Church where bones lie crisp and white
> I asked what paradise what merry sins
> Had left this little stack of jaws and shins.

XIV

From Notebook 47.

stars
bones

mell
smell

We heard the thrushes by the shore and sea
And saw the golden stars nativity
Then
We came behind the rain from Murphy's inn
Across the Church where bones lie out and in
And there I asked beneath a lonely cloud
Of strange delight with one bird singing loud
~~With what new gold you'd gilded all the moon~~
~~With what new anthem raised the rivers tune~~
What change you'd wrought in graveyard land and sea
This new wild Paradise to wake for me
And if our happiness and merry sins
Would build like these a stack of jaws and shins

XV

From the same terra-cotta notebook as XIV.

We came betwe
We heard the thrushes by the shore and sea
And saw the golden stars nativity
   where relics of old happen and merry sins
      Had built a stack of thigh-bone jaw and shin
         And then I asked beneath a lonely cloud   men
Bones from passed aged ~~by~~ from the stink of flesh

Then on we went above the Church of Glerin
Where white bones through the grass lie out and in
And there I asked beneath a lonely cloud
Of strange delight with one bird singing loud
What nights of paradise what merry sins
Had built this stack of thigh-bones jaws and shins

What new oblivion flows about from you
That Till we forgot our bones would
Till we forgot what whiten too——

119

XVI

From file marked 'Reserved Poems (Duplicates) 1906–1908 and Earlier'.

> *Then round we went the lane by Thomas Flynn*
> *Across the church where bones lie out and in*
> *and then I asked beneath a lonely*
>
> We heard the thrushes by the shore and sea,
>   *golden*
> And saw the ~~early~~ stars nativity,
> And then I asked beneath a lonely cloud
> Of strange delight, with one bird singing loud,
>   *graveyard rock*
> What change you'd wrought in ~~all this land~~ and sea
>   *wild*
> This new ~~cold~~ paradise to wake for me . . .
>
> But when we reached the high and stony site
> Of Tulla's Church where bones lie crisp and white
> *Yet knew no more than these*
> ~~I asked what paradise, what~~ merry sins,
> Had built this ~~little~~ stack of jaws and shins
>   *thigh-bones*
>
>   J. M.

XVII

There is no manuscript authority for the final version other than version XVI. The version printed in the Maunsel Edition differs from XVI in the use of 'there' instead of the MS.'s 'then' in line 5, and 'those' instead of the MS.'s 'these' in line 9. In the absence of any further evidence, and in the belief that XVI has some advantages over the Maunsel version, particularly in referring to '*these* sins', and thus to the lovers' happiness, as ending in dead bones, I have chosen to amend the accepted text.

APPENDIX C

THE SOURCE OF 'THE LADY O'CONOR' AND SYNGE'S TREATMENT OF IT

The story of Lady O'Conor appears in *The Aran Islands* on pages 18–24 of the first edition. It runs as follows:

There were two farmers in County Clare. One had a son, and the other, a fine rich man, had a daughter.

The young man was wishing to marry the girl, and his father told him to try and get her if he thought well, though a power of gold would be wanting to get the like of her.

'I will try,' said the young man.

He put all his gold into a bag. Then he went over to the other farm, and threw in the gold in front of him.

'Is that all gold?' said the father of the girl.

'All gold,' said O'Conor (the young man's name was O'Conor).

'It will not weigh down my daughter,' said the father.

'We'll see that,' said O'Conor.

Then they put them in the scales, the daughter in one side and the gold in the other. The girl went down against the ground, so O'Conor took his bag and went out on the road.

As he was going along he came to where there was a little man, and he standing with his back against the wall.

'Where are you going with the bag?' said the little man.

'Going home,' said O'Conor.

'Is it gold you might be wanting?' said the man.

'It is, surely,' said O'Conor.

'I'll give you what you are wanting,' said the man, 'and we can bargain in this way—you'll pay me back in a year the gold I give you, or you'll pay me with five pounds cut off your own flesh.'

That bargain was made between them. The man gave a bag of gold to O'Conor, and he went back with it, and was married to the young woman.

They were rich people, and he built her a grand castle on the cliffs of Clare, with a window that looked out straightly over the wild ocean.

One day when he went up with his wife to look out over the wild ocean, he saw a ship coming in on the rocks, and no sails on her at all. She was wrecked on the rocks, and it was tea that was in her, and fine silk.

O'Conor and his wife went down to look at the wreck, and when the lady O'Conor saw the silk she said she wished a dress of it.

They got the silk from the sailors, and when the Captain came up to get

121

the money for it, O'Conor asked him to come again and take his dinner with them. They had a grand dinner, and they drank after it, and the Captain was tipsy. While they were still drinking, a letter came to O'Conor, and it was in the letter that a friend of his was dead, and that he would have to go away on a long journey. As he was getting ready the Captain came to him.

'Are you fond of your wife?' said the Captain.

'I am fond of her,' said O'Conor.

'Will you make me a bet of twenty guineas no man comes near her while you'll be away on the journey?' said the Captain.

'I will bet it,' said O'Conor; and he went away.

There was an old hag who sold small things on the road near the castle, and the lady O'Conor allowed her to sleep up in her room in a big box. The Captain went down on the road to the old hag.

'For how much will you let me sleep one night in your box?' said the Captain.

'For no money at all would I do such a thing,' said the hag.

'For ten guineas?' said the Captain.

'Not for ten guineas,' said the hag.

'For twelve guineas?' said the Captain.

'Not for twelve guineas,' said the hag.

'For fifteen guineas,' said the Captain.

'For fifteen I will do it,' said the hag.

Then she took him up and hid him in the box. When night came the lady O'Conor walked up into her room, and the Captain watched her through a hole that was in the box. He saw her take off her two rings and put them on a kind of a board that was over her head like a chimney-piece, and take off her clothes, except her shift, and go up into her bed.

As soon as she was asleep the Captain came out of his box, and he had some means of making a light, for he lit the candle. He went over to the bed where she was sleeping without disturbing her at all, or doing any bad thing, and he took the two rings off the board, and blew out the light, and went down again into the box.

When O'Conor came back the Captain met him, and told him that he had been a night in his wife's room, and gave him the two rings.

O'Conor gave him the twenty guineas of the bet. Then he went up into the castle, and he took his wife up to look out of the window over the wild ocean. While she was looking he pushed her from behind, and she fell down over the cliff into the sea.

An old woman was on the shore, and she saw her falling. She went down then to the surf and pulled her out all wet and in great disorder, and she took the wet clothes off of her, and put on some old rags belonging to herself.

When O'Conor had pushed his wife from the window he went away into the land.

After a while the lady O'Conor went out searching for him, and when she had gone here and there a long time in the country, she heard that he was reaping in a field with sixty men.

She came to the field and she wanted to go in, but the gate-man would not open the gate for her. Then the owner came by, and she told him her story. He brought her in, and her husband was there, reaping, but he never gave any sign of knowing her. She showed him to the owner, and he made the man come out and go with his wife.

Then the lady O'Conor took him out on the road where there were horses, and they rode away.

When they came to the place where O'Conor had met the little man, he was there on the road before them.

'Have you my gold on you?' said the man.

'I have not,' said O'Conor.

'Then you'll pay me the flesh off your body,' said the man.

They went into a house, and a knife was brought, and a clean white cloth was put on the table, and O'Conor was put upon the cloth.

Then the little man was going to strike the lancet into him, when says lady O'Conor—

'Have you bargained for five pounds of flesh?'

'For five pounds of flesh,' said the man.

'Have you bargained for any drop of his blood?' said lady O'Conor.

'For no blood,' said the man.

'Cut out the flesh,' said lady O'Conor, 'but if you spill one drop of his blood I'll put that through you.' And she put a pistol to his head.

The little man went away and they saw no more of him.

When they got home to their castle they made a great supper, and they invited the Captain and the old hag, and the old woman that had pulled the lady O'Conor out of the sea.

After they had eaten well the lady O'Conor began, and she said they would all tell their stories. Then she told how she had been saved from the sea, and how she had found her husband.

Then the old woman told her story, the way she had found the lady O'Conor wet, and in great disorder, and had brought her in and put on her some old rags of her own.

The lady O'Conor asked the Captain for his story, but he said they would get no story from him. Then she took her pistol out of her pocket, and she put it on the edge of the table, and she said that any one that would not tell his story would get a bullet into him.

Then the Captain told the way he had got into the box, and come over to her bed without touching her at all, and had taken away the rings.

Then the lady O'Conor took the pistol and shot the hag through the body, and they threw her over the cliff into the sea.

That is my story.

In a Notebook of 1902 Synge worked out his plan for dramatizing this story:

SCENARIO (*O'Connor's Story*)

Fair day, big scales. Old man and his son, son asks wife. Girl and her father come in with baggage. Girl and gold weighed girl heaviest, girl goes. Old Connor goes Little man comes to O'Connor and gives him gold. Girl comes back and weighs again. Gold heaviest. Girl won. Act II.

Act II *Castle on Clare Coast*

O'Connor and wife talk in fog hear noises see ship wrecking on the rocks servant tells that the captain and crew are coming up with silk. Enter Captain. Silks shown, tables laid, feasting begins messenger O'Connor says he must go. Exit Lady O'Connor and Captain talk bargain made—Scene II. Bedroom Captain bribes servant, enter lady Captain steals ring.

Act III *Cliff near Castle*

Room as in II. Return of Connor. Captain shows him ring. Connor throws wife into sea out of the window.

Act IV

Captain and Little man, saved by Lady O'Connor then enter Captain and explanation.

APPENDIX D

A LATER (?) VERSION OF 'DANNY'

Although Synge submitted this poem initially as a part of his Cuala Press collection, the only typescript which corresponds to the printed version does not appear to have been made by Synge. Moreover, in this typescript, the third line of the sixth verse was typed as

> Out lepped a score and seven men

This was altered by a manuscript correction not in Synge's hand to the more logical statement of the accepted version.

There is, however, another corrected typescript, which appears to be a later version of the poem, in that the manuscript corrections make alterations to lines which exist in the accepted text.

As Synge must have furnished a neat copy for the Cuala Press, however, and as this copy may well have been made use of by Yeats in editing the Maunsel edition of the poems, it would be unwise to state that the accepted text is wrong. Nevertheless, between the time he submitted his Cuala typescript and the time of his death, Synge did have plenty of time to revise the poem. The following version must, therefore, be considered as a possible (if not probable) later version.

> One night a score of Erris men,
> A score I'm told and nine,
> Said, 'We'll get shut of Danny's noise
> Of girls and widows dying.
>
> 'There's not his like from Binghamstown
> To Boyle and Ballycroy,
> At playing hell on decent girls,
> At skelping man and boy.
>
> 'He's left two pairs of female twins
> Beyond in Killacreest,
> And twice in Crosmolina fair
> He's struck the parish priest,
>
> 'But we'll confound him in the night
> A mile beyond the mullet
> Ten will quench his bloody sight,
> And ten will choke his gullet.'

It wasn't long till Danny came,
  From Bangor making way.
He was damning moon and stars
  And whistling grand and gay.

Then in a gap of Hazel Glen
  Where not a rabbit stared
Out rose the nine and twenty men
  Without a whispering word.

Then Danny smashed the nose on Byrne
  He split the lips on three
And bit across the right hand thumb
  Of one Red Shawn Magee

But seven tripped him up behind,
  And seven kicked before,
And seven squeezed around his throat
  Till Danny kicked no more.

But some destroyed him with their heels,
  Some tramped him in the mud,
Some stole his purse and timber pipe,
  And some washed off his blood.

Now when youre walking out the way
  From Bangor to Belmullet,
You'll see a flat cross on a stone
  Where men choked Danny's gullet.

There is an alternative version of the first line of the last verse,
which reads:

  And when you've walked a league of way.

INDEX OF FIRST LINES

I. POEMS

Still south I went and west and south again, 32.
The chiffchaff and the celandine, 54.
There's snow in every street, 63.
Though trees have many a flake, 42.
Thrice cruel fell my fate, 13.
Thrush, linnet, stare and wren, 48.
Today you have tutored and healed my head, 25.
We heard the thrushes by the shore and sea, 55.
We met among the furze in golden mist, 43.
We reached the Glen of Thrushes where Usheen, 45.
Wet winds and rain are in the street, 16.
What records will this new year write, 7.
When your hour was rung at last, 21.
With Fifteen-ninety or Sixteen-sixteen, 33.
You are a peasant, mere maid by the day, 29.
You are my God and my Heaven, 22.
You squirrel, angel eel and bat, 65.
You've plucked a curlew, drawn a hen, 35.

II. TRANSLATIONS

Ah, Death, is it you that have left the world, 96.
Are you bearing in mind that time, 81.
How many times, running away from all people, 99.
If I had thought that the voice of my grief, 101.
If the birds are making lamentation, 89.
I'm getting old in your big house, 82.
I'm growing old with singing on your stairs, 83.
I never set my two eyes on a head was so fine, 84.
In the years of her age the most beautiful, 88.
Is this the nest in which my Phoenix, 94.
I was never anyplace where I saw so clearly, 98.
Let you go down, sorrowful rhymes, 95.
Life is flying from me, 86.
Mother of God that's Lady of the Heavens, 79.
My flowery and green age was passing away, 93.
Oh our poor Judas, what is it you've done, 85.
Sweet spirit, you that do be coming down, 100.
The eyes that I would be talking of so warmly, 90.
The first day she passed up and down, 97.
The man I had a love for—a great rascal, 80.
There was one time maybe, 102.
The south wind is coming back, 92.
What a grudge I am bearing the earth, 91.
What is it you're thinking, lonesome heart?, 87.

J. M. Synge died in 1909 and *The Works of John M. Synge* was
published in four volumes by Maunsel & Co., Dublin, in 1910.
Since that time, with the exception of a few minor verses and one
or two fragments of prose, the canon of his work has remained
unaltered. Nevertheless, much unpublished material exists, for
the most part of great interest and significance for the
understanding of Synge's methods of work and development. This
material, including early drafts of the plays, note-books, poems,
and fragments of poetic drama, has now been thoroughly explored
in order to create this definitive edition which not only collects
together all that is of significance in his printed and in his unprinted
work, but also, by a careful use of worksheets and early drafts,
indicates much of the process of creation which occurred before
the production of the printed page.

The *Collected Works* is in four volumes, under the general
editorship of Professor Robin Skelton, of the University of Victoria,
British Columbia, who begins the series with his edition of the
poems and translations, in which he has more than doubled the
canon of Synge's verse. The prefaces by W. B. Yeats and Synge to
the first, Cuala Press, edition, are also included. The late Dr. Alan
Price, of Queen's University, Belfast, edited the prose and
Professor Ann Saddlemyer, of Victoria College, University of
Toronto, has edited the plays, published in two volumes. Originally
published by Oxford University Press, and now published by
arrangement with them, the volumes of the *Collected Works* are
also available in hardcover bindings.

Cover design by James Gillison.
Cover picture: sketch of J. M. Synge at Coole, by Jack B. Yeats,
reproduced by kind permission of Michael B. Yeats and
Anne Yeats.

Colin Smythe Ltd., Gerrards Cross, Buckinghamshire
0-86140-134-4 Hbk and 0-86140-058-5 Pbk

The Catholic University of America Press, Washington, D.C.
0-8132-0563-8 Hbk and 0-8132-0562-X Pbk